CW01512773

IT'S A
SCORCHER!

Also by William McInnes

A Man's Got to Have a Hobby

Cricket Kings

The Making of Modern Australia

(with Essential Media & Entertainment)

That'd Be Right

Worse Things Happen at Sea (with Sarah Watt)

The Laughing Clowns

The Birdwatcher

Holidays

Full Bore

Fatherhood

Christmas Tales

Yeah, Nah!

WILLIAM McINNES

IT'S A SCORCHER!

TALES OF THE AUSTRALIAN SUMMER

hachette
AUSTRALIA

These are my memories. The names and descriptions of some people have been changed so that they too can preserve their own memories, in their own ways.

William McInnes

 hachette
AUSTRALIA

Published in Australia and New Zealand in 2025
by Hachette Australia
(an imprint of Hachette Australia Pty Limited)
Gadigal Country, Level 17, 207 Kent Street, Sydney, NSW 2000
www.hachette.com.au

Hachette Australia acknowledges and pays our respects to the past and present
Traditional Owners and Custodians of Country throughout Australia
and recognises the continuation of cultural, spiritual and educational practices
of Aboriginal and Torres Strait Islander peoples. Our head office is located on
the lands of the Gadigal people of the Eora Nation.

Copyright © William McInnes 2025

This book is copyright. Apart from any fair dealing for the purposes of private study,
research, criticism or review permitted under the *Copyright Act 1968*, no part
may be stored or reproduced by any process without prior written permission.
Enquiries should be made to the publisher.

 A catalogue record for this
book is available from the
National Library of Australia

ISBN: 978 0 7336 5291 2 (paperback)

Cover design by Christabella Designs
Cover photograph courtesy of Getty Images
Author photo courtesy of Claudia Scalzi
Typeset in 12.7/20 pt Bembo Std by Bookhouse, Sydney
Printed and bound in Australia by McPherson's Printing Group

 MIX
Paper from
responsible sources
FSC® C001695

The paper this book is printed on is certified against the
Forest Stewardship Council® Standards. McPherson's Printing
Group holds FSC® chain of custody certification SA-COC-005379.
FSC® promotes environmentally responsible, socially beneficial
and economically viable management of the world's forests.

To everyone who has lived and will live through an Australian summer.

CONTENTS

1

A WALK ALONG A JETTY

Early mornings make me think of certain things. One of those things is my mother. And her pistol. My mother was very good with her pistol. Her aim was true, she had a sure hand and certainly never missed — which was unfortunate for me, for I was always her target. I wasn't hard to miss for I was almost always asleep, or at the very least in the midst of some half-hearted attempt to wake myself up.

One summer holidays in my middle teens my mother decided that I was too keen for a lie-in and was 'Sleeping your life away!'

She began by roaring at me in the early mornings. 'Wake up. Wake up! You're sleeping your life away, you stupid boy!'

My brother was some years older than me and had been a definite log in the mornings, but my mother swore he was nothing compared to me.

'He hibernated, but you, you are mummified. Get up, get up from your sarcophagus, you swine.'

I had no doubt that my parents loved me. They loved all their children and we loved them. They just had a rather offhand way of dealing with us. And even though they loved us deeply, they would also quite happily throttle us at particular times. Sometimes, to put it frankly, we were a bit much, and they had other things they wanted to get on with.

What those things were was never really apparent to me back then though. It seemed to be grown-up stuff. Like yelling at mowers that wouldn't work, shouting at the dogs, muttering 'Where are my bloody keys', definitely getting round to phoning so-and-so about something important and then never actually managing to do anything of the sort, or perhaps walking around ruminating.

'I'm just going to walk the estate for a ruminate,' my father would say, and off he'd go around his 'estate' – our battleaxe block on the Redcliffe Peninsula. Around the yard and down the drive and back again.

My mother also adopted the term and would sit in a garden chair looking down at a pot of mint with her head tilted to one side. If you interrupted her, she would roar, 'Go away, I'm ruminating.'

I'm sure my parents did other things too, but understanding all of that was beyond me at the time. And, anyway, it was their business. And they weren't fond of making their business our business.

One thing I did know was that one of the great irritants in my parents' lives was having to get their brood of children out of bed.

'*We* are not your bleeding alarm clocks!' was my father's opinion. 'You want to get out of bed early then buy yourself a rooster and let him cock-a-doodle-doodle in your earhole!' My father waved off certain parental duties, including the act of resurrection. 'You lot are worse than bloody Lazarus, nobody will be rolling away your stone anytime soon.'

So, it was left to my mother to get us out of bed.

Five children into parenthood, my mother had had a gutful of attending to her chicks by the time I was a teenager.

My three sisters were not as tardy as we two boys and they required only a few hearty bellows to get them up and going or, on difficult days, a few ominous threats. These were rather theatrically delivered by my mother, who seemed to enjoy intoning, 'Do we need a glass of tossed aqua?'

But for we boys, threats gave way to action. My older brother and I shared a bedroom so I had seen my mother's wake-up tactics at close range.

My brother, the hibernating log, had indeed required the odd glass of water to be thrown at him to get him up and out of bed.

'My God, it's alive!' I could hear my mother roar as my brother flung himself from his bed like a cross between The Three Stooges and some poor sod who had just been zapped with an incredibly powerful defibrillator.

'He's like something you'd see in a Berlin nightclub!' chortled our mum. The fact my mother had never been in, or even seen, a Berlin nightclub made the observation even funnier.

Then she would turn to me, still in my bunk, look down and sweetly say, 'Now let that be a lesson to you when your time comes.'

But, at the same time, this tossed aqua method irritated my mother.

Her water-tossing was not a targeted effort. It was more akin to area bombing by Allied aircraft in the Second World War, where precision was not guaranteed. It could be effective but there was collateral damage, and in this case it was the bedding, which needed some lengthy airing afterwards.

Being the youngest and the most spoilt, I was a tad more entombed than my brother so, when it did come to be my time, my mother downstreamed her tossed aqua technique into a plastic orange water pistol. She had bought the pistol from the Woolies Variety store in Redcliffe. It had a vague resemblance to the .44 Magnum Smith & Wesson Clint Eastwood used when he was playing Dirty Harry, the mean-eyed, tough-talking San Francisco police detective who doubled as a vigilante for justice.

Both my parents had a fondness for water pistols. My father had a yellow one, also a Woolies Variety purchase, in the shape of a Luger handgun. It was filled with kerosene and was tied to the frangipani tree next to the homemade barbecue he had erected.

This yellow Luger, he was at pains to point out, was no toy. It was tied to a branch with two knotted long white football bootlaces.

'This is not a toy – it's a utensil. Don't be touching it. It's a utensil – a barbie encourager.'

And he would take his utensil and squirt it at the budding barbecue fire and flames would erupt.

'It's the little touch of kero that does the trick,' he would say, as if he were some Stubbies-clad Jedi Knight explaining the benefits of a lightsaber. 'It's a flame enhancer.' And he'd gently wind the extended football laces back around a limb of the frangipani tree. 'Always fancied using a Luger, lovely weapon.'

Once he'd placed it back on the tree, he would say in an outrageous German accent, 'It iz not a toy! A uteenzil!'

Of course, every chance you got to use the utensil on the sly and make the barbie erupt like Krakatoa you would, but that was just part of the fun. Whenever an orange cloud briefly roared, my mum would say, 'Well, at least the smoke keeps the mozzies away.'

Her choice of storage for her orange wake-up machine — the .44 Magnum water pistol — was inside the fridge. Ice-cold water would stream from its barrel and weave its wake-up-and-out-of-bed magic at me.

It was quite something to have my blankets or sheet pulled back and to be awakened by a freezing jet of water to the melon. I'd open my eyes to see my mother towering over me. She was a tall woman with a fountain of white hair and the orange Magnum extending from her hand. Dirty Harry would have been proud, though instead of saying, 'Do you feel lucky, punk?' à la Clint Eastwood, my mother one morning said, 'Do you feel sleepy, punk?'

She was quite circumspect with her squeezing of the trigger, though occasionally she would throw back the sheets to let me have one. She might then see some signs of physical activity in my nether regions, and she'd let me have another few bursts along with the advice, 'Put that thing out before you come downstairs, dirty bits!'

It was, I must admit, a bit fun.

I once told a friend who had served in the Australian military about my mother's wake-up tactics and he laughed and said it sounded like a hazing ritual at Duntroon. 'She sounds like a drill sergeant I had there.' I assume he was joking.

My mum was impressed with the Magnum. 'It's so accurate, no need to dry the linen at all!'

She was especially pleased because the former collateral damage had implications when drying the bedding. 'Forget the House of Windsor, we looked like the House of Bedwetters.'

My father thought for a moment and said, 'If you spelt Bedwetters with a Z, it would have that ring of European royalty about it.' Then he laughed to himself and offered to my mother, 'When Eu-ro-a-pean' – he elongated the syllables to make it sound like 'when you-are-a-peein' – 'you are a Bedwetterzzzz. Von Bedwetterzzzz. German, most likely.' After a pause he added, 'Makes me want to grab my Luger.'

'Colin!' my mother yelled at him, and then laughed. For a while in our home going off to the toilet to do 'ones' was referred to as 'Off to Von Bedwetterz'.

And as things invariably evolved in the house where I grew up, Von Bedwetterz soon became the name of one of those lovely old ropey movies that would screen on an early summer Sunday arvo, just before the cricket got serious. That's how Frank Sinatra's *Von Ryan's Express* became known to us as *Von Bedwetterz Express*.

Ostensibly, the film was about prisoners of war making a daring escape, led by Frank Sinatra and his toupee in the role of tough-talking and perpetually cranky Colonel Von Ryan.

Frank's Von Ryan always appeared slightly irritated, as if he was in a hurry to get done with things and be somewhere else, the classic signs of someone who was busting. Or, in more correct English, someone who was eagerly wanting to urinate.

'He's in a rush all right,' said my mother, 'that's why he's cranky – probably wants to Von Bedwett.'

At the end of the film, Frank Von Bedwetterz, after bravely holding off a legion of Nazi troops, runs to a train with an arm outstretched, trying to pull himself aboard.

Throughout the film the bad guys had been terrible shots, spraying thousands of bullets this way and that and always missing the good guys, but miraculously the ending included the one good shot in the Wehrmacht.

Sadly, for Frank and his toupee, he was cut down by a suitably nasty pretend Nazi with a gun.

Frank and his hairpiece lay lifeless on the tracks. There was a moment's pause before some old hammy ham intoned, in a suitably fruity theatrical voiceover, 'I once told Von Ryan, if only one gets out, it's a victory!'

We never really heard that line though because my father would always fill the pause when Frank and his possum lay on the tracks. 'Well, that Jerry's certainly not using a water pistol,' he'd mutter.

'No, but he is a very good shot,' answered my mother.

Years later, during a long Christmas trip back to Redcliffe with my family, I sat with my mother in a coffee shop by the beach and Frank Sinatra's lovely voice came warbling from the café's sound system. He sang, of all things, 'Summer Wind'.

As my mother delighted herself with a cappuccino, or 'cuppa-chino' as she loved pronouncing it, she paused long enough to sigh, 'Oh here's ol' Blue eyes Bedwetterz.'

I nodded and then asked, 'Whatever happened to your pistol?'

'Oh, I threw it away. After a while you just got up by yourself at a reasonable time.'

I laughed a little.

'You know,' my mother continued, 'it was a sin, you in your tomb sleeping away the summer days. It made me furious. Summer is the time of bounty – of life to be lived, things to be done and adventures to be had. It wasn't just me being an old crank, I was trying to teach you something.'

I saw she was serious. She took a sip of her cuppa-chino and licked her lips. 'Life is to be lived, and summer is the time to live well.'

I smiled and nodded my head. 'I still like a lie-in, Mum.'

She held up her cuppa-chino and eyeballed me as if she were holding the orange plastic .44 Magnum once again. 'I can always buy another orange enhancer, you know!'

And we both laughed.

•

I woke up very early this morning. And in my mind, I could hear our laughter from that day. I thought of my mother.

I hadn't needed her orange .44 Magnum to get me out of bed this summer morning because I was on the other side of the country to where I lived. I was in Busselton, a lovely town in the south-west of Western Australia, and it was daylight savings, another thing telling me it was summer.

I looked at my watch, it was set to Eastern Standard Time, or rather Eastern Standard Time with Daylight Savings. Daylight Savings – or as my mother and Aunty Rita called it, Melbourne Time – was an alien concept that didn't belong to sensible-thinking Queenslanders.

When I moved away from Redcliffe and Queensland, any inconvenience or mix-up caused by the time difference during summer always seemed to be my fault, as if I alone was responsible. If a planned call was an hour out then it was the fault of 'your silly bleeding daylight savings'. When I once suggested that daylight savings was all about making the most of your day and should have been right up my mum's alley 'of not sleeping your life away', she'd scoff and say, 'William and his silly daylight savings, stupid boy!'

I laughed again.

My watch read eight o'clock. Pretty early in the morning for me, but the time difference of two hours and the hour of daylight saving meant my time in the West was 5 am.

Five am and no water pistol. Well done me. What to do, though? Early mornings meant sunrises, something that I didn't see that often, but when I did, I enjoyed them.

The first time I was aware of the power of a sunrise was during an exquisitely ridiculous army cadet camp I was a part of during my high school years. The camp was held in late February, on the last weekend of summer.

It was a collection of ungainly and unsure adolescents in ill-fitting uniforms being yelled at by teachers in uniforms pretending to be captains and majors. There was awful food, too many insects and something called 'picket duty'.

Two of us army cadets had to perform picket duty outside a vast canopy that had been decreed a 'barracks' by a maths teacher who was an imaginary major. Picket duty involved walking around the perimeter of this ungainly marquee, which the previous weekend had been used for a wedding reception by the niece of the economics teacher who was a pretend captain. Having an eye for a bargain and the keen sense of a dollar saved, Captain Economics had snapped up the marquee for the cadet camp at a good price.

As the canvas flapped and billowed in the night wind, groaning like some great beast with indigestion, two guards performed picket duty while holding sticks of dowel timber as if they were rifles. We were told to carry our 'bang sticks' correctly at all times.

I think the idea was that we learned how to treat things with respect and caution, carrying our dowel weapon with its muzzle resting against our shoulder and the butt cradled in our palms. There was even a red line to indicate the pointy end of the dowel weapon, and woe betide any cadet who walked around with the muzzle in their palm.

If you were caught carrying your weapon the wrong way you had to do ten push-ups and then jump up in the air ten times with your arms folded.

It was all quite silly, really.

Especially when a creature called Armstrong and I were the allotted guards for the last shift of the night and we staggered around in the dark tripping over ourselves. Near the end of our graveyard shift, Armstrong – who was quite an odd lad from out west and had the habit of emitting sounds that resembled some odd animated character speaking a made-up language – walked as if in a daze.

He had a throaty growl for a voice and had tried to keep himself awake by singing, an experience which was fraught because the pretend officer teachers would shriek from their comfortable bunks, 'Shut up! No singing on picket duty!' Then they would mutter amongst themselves.

'It's that idiot again.'

'Is he sleepwalking?'

'No idea, but he sounds like a zombie.'

'Will this marquee hold? It feels like it's going to take off.'

'I got it for a cracking price, that's why we've coin left over for the social club.'

'No singing on picket duty! Is he in pain?'

'He's singing a song from *The Muppets*.'

'Muppets?'

'That manumma numma song.'

They were referring to the song by the Italian composer Piero Umiliani entitled 'Mah Na Mah Na' that was popularised by *The Muppets* TV show, where puppet creatures almost as odd as Armstrong performed the song.

Actually, Armstrong was trying to sing a song by Pussyfoot, a redhead also known as Donna Jones, who warbled something called 'The Way That You Do It'.

It got progressively worse near the end of the song because Armstrong had completely given up the ghost, Pussyfooting away in some sort of satanic growl and tripping over his firearm. Namely his bit of dowel.

A biology teacher who was pretending to be a lieutenant had obviously had enough and reprimanded Armstrong, who was now rather jauntily flicking his dowel here and there as if he were doing some old-time dance number.

When he tapped his giggle-hatted head with the end of the dowel the biology lieutenant curtly put him in his place.

'Armstrong!'

Armstrong gutturally Pussyfooted back.

'That is no way to treat a firearm!'

Armstrong sounded gutturally surprised as he Pussyfooted in response.

I wasn't sure whether he was still singing or trying to speak, but it sounded like a cross between a drunken monk attempting a Gregorian chant and Linda Blair from *The Exorcist*.

'Your firearm, your bang stick!' said the exasperated teacher. 'You could have blown your head off!'

I was standing to attention, my broomstick dowel held correctly and my eyes staring steadfastly ahead, and so expected to now hear the grunts of Armstrong performing push-ups and leaping in the air with arms folded like some mad Russian dancer.

Instead, there was a pause and then the only words I ever really heard Armstrong say in any decipherable way. He growled out a slow-motion and stupefied, 'It's a piece of fucking dowel!'

There was a pause, and the biology teacher tried to stifle a laugh before he sent Armstrong off to bed.

The biology teacher was quite a nice man and when he approached me he was still trying not to laugh.

'Sir!' I stood to attention and presented my firearm.

He laughed again. 'Good firearm safety,' he said. And he winked.

He looked to the sky and then gestured for me to follow him up a small rise. 'Here,' he said, stopping and looking up at the brightening sky.

'Sunrise. Never get to see that many, really,' he said, 'but it's a treat when you do. Special moment, the beginning of a day. Just think of the endless possibility that lies ahead.'

He paused. When he spoke again it was like he had forgotten he was a teacher. He was just a bloke who wanted to share something, without the air of a figure of authority, even in his pretend officer's uniform.

'Think about all those people who've gone before and seen a sunrise. We're sharing that with them, but this is our sunrise.' He held his hand out a bit and then pushed the air away, as if he were a little embarrassed.

'And it's always nice to get a chance to start again or at the very least see what you can make of the new day.'

We stood in silence and watched as light crept across the sky in the way that it had done so many times before, before so many different sets of human eyes, but this was our sunrise now, my sunrise.

It was lovely.

And then he asked me for my firearm, smiled again and nodded goodbye.

•

I sat up on my bed and looked through the hotel room's window. Busselton. Waiting outside was a jetty and the ocean and a sunrise on a summer's day.

I have a friend from Perth who says the sunsets of the West Australian landscape are the treasures of the day, for the sun sets the water and sky ablaze with colours that streak across the ceiling of the day. Breathtaking, she told me. So grand

and gorgeous that when you see them you feel somewhere in yourself, in your heart or soul, that time is passing and the beauty before you reminds you to live.

I don't doubt that, but when I asked about the sunrises she shrugged her shoulders. 'Bit bland really,' was her opinion.

I laughed as I pulled on some clothes and made my way down to the jetty. A bit bland? I decided to see for myself.

Already there were people about, all up early without the aid of a time difference and daylight savings to help them. They were walking along the foreshore, or the jetty, a long thin finger that bends slightly as it stretches out over the water. Somebody once told me quite proudly that it's one of the longest jetties in the world and the longest wooden-piled jetty in the Southern Hemisphere.

I'm sure that's impressive, but it's also quite endearing that Australians still like to rate ourselves and our achievements in terms of 'the Southern Hemisphere', as if we shouldn't try to compete with the serious folk up there in the Northern Hemisphere.

And I wondered if other people in the world ever called such a structure a jetty. Didn't those Northern Hemisphere types say piers or docks?

It didn't really matter; a jetty is exactly what the structure that snaked out over the waters of Geographe Bay was and Busselton was rightly proud of it.

After the jetty was decommissioned in the early 1970s it was marked for demolition, but the local community saved it and imbued it with character, almost a tangible emotional attachment.

It's been tarted up over the years, with a visitor centre and novelty train ride out to an underwater observatory. And its precinct on the foreshore has a series of breweries and restaurants, as well as the spanking hotel I'd woken up in and a convention centre that tourist flyers say makes Busselton an event destination.

I looked back at the new buildings. An event centre. The town had just hosted 'Schoolies', the week-long celebration for secondary school students who have formally completed their education.

Across the globe, the beginning of summer occurs at the end of the school year and then the rest of summer is that lotus land, the time to enjoy and ride through till your education continues on its next stage or you enter adulthood and what-ever career you seek to engage in.

Those Northern Hemisphere folk, though, have their summer in the middle months. In Australia our summer is the time of endings and beginnings, for the calendar ticks over to the New Year one third of the way through the season.

It seemed to me that added a heightened sense of time passing and of life turning over through our summer. What that might mean I couldn't quite put into words, but it gave me a nagging sentimental pall. All those students who had left school and now waited to begin their lives as adults.

The jetty was filled mostly with fisher folk or those starting the day with a bit of exercise.

Those fishing seemed inordinately happy for some reason, offering nods of welcome and 'g'days'. Perhaps it was enough to be doing something they loved.

The sky above began to change slowly. Not bland at all, I thought, more a subtle encroaching change, almost imperceptible.

The biology teacher had spoken of the possibility of the day all those summers ago and it seemed to me that within the hearts of the fisher folk the possibility of a big catch was ripe.

Whiting, tailor, sometimes snapper, herring, skippy – a form of trevally – and, at night, squid are all popular catches off that jetty.

Summer, my mum had said, was a time of bounty, and the people who fished here were ready to fill their baskets.

I walked past a cleaning station and the scales of a recent catch littered the jetty and caught the gentle light in the sky. The scales seemed to glow almost like sequins, reminding me of confetti at a wedding.

A father and his young son walked up beside me and then past. 'Now you be careful with that rod,' the father said, 'hold it properly.' And the little boy nodded and held the rod for all he was worth, walking with a sure and steady tread, almost at a ceremonial pace that imbued the trek out to fish with a great dignity, as if he were the sergeant-at-arms carrying the mace into Parliament.

The rod was a pretty basic piece of equipment, but it meant everything to that little boy. The father winked at me as they walked on, and they stopped not far from the spot where I wanted to take in the sunrise.

The spot where there were plaques of remembrance. They were to people whose ashes had been scattered into the water below. The plaques held simple words, boldly engraved on brass plates fastened onto the boards. I had walked to this part of the jetty many times before and had never failed to be moved by the words. They could be mundane and ordinary yet they had a beauty too. I didn't know the people whose life and character were caught in these few words but I felt closer to them, to their essence, each time I stood on this jetty.

You can redevelop buildings and foreshores and even jetties, but you can't redevelop the essence of a place. The part of it that breathes humanity. You should cherish such a place. You can fish from it, walk along it, but it's not just a bit of functionary infrastructure, it breathes.

I read some of the plaques.

A man of great pride
Who left a lasting impression

Now catching the fish
He never caught.

An independent woman with a great zest for life
Now with her loving husband Jim
This loving couple will now travel through the blue waters.

I felt that sad sting of melancholy that pierces you even on a lovely morning.

A final plaque read simply, 'Still swimming in the bay.'

It was these words that caught me, as they had the other times I have stood out here above the water. I looked at the bay below and thought of those I had loved and sometimes barely knew. My parents. My father – a man of great pride who indeed had left a lasting impression. My mother – an independent woman with a great zest for life.

My first child, who died at birth and never drew breath. And my wife.

It was my wife who I thought of that morning, for she loved the summer and the water. She wrote once, 'I can't be sure when or where my love of the water – watching it, being in it, painting it – began. But I can't imagine it ever being unimportant to me. I love its cycle, moving from rivers and oceans to clouds then rain, tides linking to the phases of the moon and the moon to the stars. If I can't figure out what everything else in the world is about, I can always be calmed by the simultaneous predictability and unpredictability of water and the weather. Walking along a beach is the most soothing thing I can do.'

In the water she felt as fast and smooth as a seal or a penguin. She loved it; loved so many things about it. Being weightless, unwatched. She felt graceful as she dived beneath its surface and curved like a dolphin through the deep, before pushing off and leaping out of the water briefly to dive back under to the quiet.

I stood and, for a moment, despite all that I have, for the fortunate life I have led, all I could feel was what I had lost.

I let out a sound and felt very alone.

But I wasn't alone. I heard a voice. I turned and it was the little boy with his fishing rod. He still held it very deliberately but now he was looking up at me.

Perhaps I had made a louder sound than I had meant; perhaps he could see, in that moment, how stricken I was.

'Are you all right?' he said.

His father was not far away. 'You good, mate?' He nodded.

You must never underestimate the ability of people to be kind and generous and to think outside themselves.

I nodded back. 'Yeah, all good, just having a ruminate,' and I pointed to the plaques.

The father took in the brass plates and the water and nodded again. 'Yeah, can get to you out here, even when the fish run.'

I nodded again. Why is it, I thought to myself, that when men are slightly emotional, we nod a lot. That at least made me smile.

'He's a good little man you've got there,' I said to the father.

He nodded again. 'Yeah, he's not too bad – although he was up bloody early this morning.'

'Got to get up early to catch the fish and to beat the heat,' said the little boy.

We both laughed and the father said, 'You had to blast me out of bed but here we are.'

I laughed and wondered whether any orange Magnums were involved. I didn't think so.

'He's right, the young fella,' the father continued, 'it's going to be bloody hot today. First belter of summer. It's a scorcher.'

I nodded, again, and turned to start walking back to my hotel.

Jetties are funny structures; you walk along them to their end, and you are left standing above a place where you can go no further. There was a metaphor for life somewhere in that, if I could have been bothered to make sense of it, but as I looked back, I also looked forward to this time of bounty, to the endless possibility of the day ahead.

I decided that I liked the sunrises in the West very much.

It was a long walk back. I hadn't realised that I had gone so far, but that was all right. Sometimes when you look back, you realise that those who have left are still with you when you remember them. Remembering those summer days, the people, the events and the stories is what this book is about.

I tried to walk a little quicker. It was going to be a scorcher.

2

IT'S ONLY THREE MONTHS

Summer only lasts three months. Well, any season only lasts three months but so much fuss is made over summer, especially here in Australia, that sometimes those three months can matter a lot more than they probably should. There's a lot going on – there's Christmas, New Year, school breakups, school holidays, family holidays. It's a floating time where days disappear and you can easily forget the date and even what day it might be.

The whole country seems to shut down for about four weeks and only gets going again at the end of January when school returns and people head back into the 'real' world.

If intergalactic supreme beings ever wanted to invade Australia this would be the time to do it because every decent

Australian would simply look at the calendar and say to themselves, 'We'll take a gander at it and maybe sort it out after the end of January.'

The last month of summer, February, is usually the time given over to easing back into whatever we are supposed to be doing with ourselves: work, education or fighting off Martians who've read *The War of the Worlds* and have had a few ideas.

Then it is time to get serious, for the summer, the time of living high, is done.

Until then there is too much to occupy our summer selves. There are events! All with an exclamation mark added to stress their importance.

The Boxing Day Test! The Australian Open Tennis! The Sydney to Hobart Yacht Race! Festivals galore! Blockbusters in cinemas! New Year's Eve fireworks!

In summer, everybody in Australia tries to find something iconic from which to launch rockets, flares and all sorts of igniting colour. Why anybody tries to compete with Sydney and their fireworks night of nights is beyond me, except it seems to be an Australian tradition to try to outdo Sydney.

I've lost count of the number of times I was asked to host a wonderfully haphazard carols night held in the Yarraville Gardens in Melbourne, which was run by the wonderfully haphazard Ron Palmer.

Ron was a ceaseless source of good humour and good citizenship. A wonderful old coot who was a reminder of the best of a different Australia.

He seemed to have gone to kindy with Moses, he'd been around that long. He'd served throughout the Second World War in the RAAF, flying missions around the skies in a Beaufort bomber, and when he returned after 'the shindig' (Ron's words), he assumed that Australia would muddle along just as it had before – roughly about seven million people, nearly all white Anglo Australians, operating as an outpost of the Empire.

But Australia changed dramatically, and Ron became, to me, a wonderful example of how someone from an older generation could embrace the changing face of Australia.

He had a generosity born through a sense of service and he never took himself seriously. And his laugh. A great howl of delight. He'd throw his head back and laugh with his whole soul. Three people I know have laughed like that: Ron, my dad and my son.

It is a sound that makes me happy.

When I told Ron that, of course he let out a howl. 'Don't talk claptrap, son.'

Then he winked and gave me a nod.

One night in the gardens, with the temperature at almost 40 degrees, I heard that laugh. I asked Ron what was amusing him.

He put his hand on my shoulder. 'I love this bloody country, boy. Look at that bloke there,' he said, pointing to an African Australian man, 'asking that bloke there,' pointing to a Vietnamese Australian man, 'to move a bit so he can video that bloke up there,' he pointed to a Chinese Australian man on stage, 'singing "*White* Christmas" on a boiling night like this. Bloody magnificent!'

When the fireworks went off over the Maribyrnong River and exploded over the giant dock cranes that kids always said looked like big giraffes, he laughed again. He was standing with his head turned to the sky.

'Bloody magnificent! Sydney can go stick its bungers and fizzers! We've got our giraffes! What a night. What a bloody night!'

I laughed. Kids seemed to come in all ages on that night in Yarraville Gardens.

Every New Year's Eve the National Broadcaster screens the festivities from Sydney at the Opera House on that lovely harbour, while the bridge is festooned with glowing red and blue fireworks that manage to make an amazingly beautiful piece of civic engineering look like the lights of a police car on pursuit.

And when the gushy talking heads begin to wax lyrical about 'Where else would you rather be to watch this spectacle?' I hear a lovely sound.

I hear Ron's laugh and I think of him — a glorious ordinary man who gave so much to his community. And I think of how well a life can be lived. So thanks for that, Sydney.

Sydney is okay. I kind of like that, even when it's constantly tearing itself down and rebuilding itself, however chaotic and frenetic it may seem, it's always Sydney. The sort of place that, in the parlance of my parents, has tickets on itself. You could organise the Second Coming at your fireworks night, with the Son of God wandering around the Catherine wheels waving a couple of sparklers, and people in the Emerald City would still say, 'Yes, you've got Jesus, which is a good get, but you don't have the bridge or the Opera House or the harbour.'

The first half of summer also has concerts! And festivals! Everywhere you look! If you are not out and about and living life at — what did my mother call it? 'A time of bounty' — then you are not living at all. Cue a blast of tossed aqua from a large water pistol.

Summer is also the time of natural events, the festival of weather if you like.

One of my favourite images of the Australian summer is a photo of such remarkable imagery and power that I believe it sums up how we see ourselves as a nation or perhaps how we would like to see ourselves. It's a photo taken by Mark Williams of a cricket club match where players pay scant attention to what appears to be a raging bushfire just behind them. The only player who seems to notice is the batsman who isn't on strike. He slouches on his bat with one hand on his hip. Of course, he doesn't wear a helmet, just a peaked cap. And he has the air of not being so much worried but slightly interested. As if the fire might be something to chat about at the drinks break.

It's a poster for the summer festival of disaster.

Floods, fires and cyclones. The holy trinity for newspapers, electronic and digital media. These are invariably referred to as DISASTERS! by gushy media types. And sometimes they truly are, but the media can also make a mountain out of a molehill in their eagerness to harvest exclamation marks to match the exclamation mark season.

Dorothea Mackellar wrote about Australia being a land of drought and flooding, so acute natural events have been around since time immemorial, but there are more people in areas where they weren't before and human inhabitants, colonisation, industrialisation and growing human activity can all add to the 'natural' effects of one of Dorothea's droughts, fires or floods.

I was waiting on a train station in Melbourne recently when I noticed amongst the tags, swear words and bubble-writing graffiti, a riff on Dorothea Mackellar's 'My Country', written in Sharpie pen.

I live in a sunburnt country

A land of solar screen plains

of ridiculous renewable targets

and unbelievable nuclear power claims

Perhaps Dorothea Mackellar could have come up with a few rhyming stanzas to tackle the climate change debate for I'm sure it would be a tad more graceful than the way some people carry on when a microphone is in front of their mouth.

But no doubt the naysayers, who seem to be the loudest voices in the argument, and the ten-minutes-after-midnight doomsayers would only continue to bang on and on and on.

There is one man-made disaster of the summer months that nobody can defend or doubt, a disaster that echoes through the years and haunts the memory of those who were unfortunate enough to witness it. Even some of the perpetrators of the said act will carry the shadow of their decisions deep within their souls, where it lies dormant and then rises to their consciousness, usually followed by a shriek of embarrassment and shame.

And still yet other perpetrators wander through life blissfully unaware of their deeds. They may well be recidivist offenders.

This man-made disaster, most often seen in summer, is of course swimwear choices.

Depending on where you come from in Australia these items of attire can be called swimmers, togs, bathers or cozzies. All Australians know what these terms mean and how these garments, especially during the summer months, can be the source of serious crimes of human vanity resulting in crimes against humanity.

Perhaps a brief history of swimwear may help us. The ancient Egyptians loved taking a dip in the Nile and sometimes wore shifts or jumped into the water in their altogether. The Romans had bathhouses where apparently blokes could jump in and lather up in the rubbity. Women could do the same, although some coverings were thought best for morality.

Ah, morality.

Apparently during the Renaissance, a high point of creativity and thinking, swimming was widely discouraged. Bright idea, Leonardo.

In the ensuing centuries people began dipping their toe back in and then immersing more of their body. However, when they did this they were more often than not covered in heavy garments made from everything from wool to canvas.

Talk about bad chaffing prospects.

These garments could be weighted down to stop them from floating up and therefore stop the possibility of any more of the wearer's body being visible. The wearers, of course, were almost always women.

Subsequent developments in swimwear have been a result of the clash between a desire for increasing fluidity and comfort and the varying morality views of the day.

This was exemplified by the furore around Australian Annette Kellerman's swimwear.

When Captain Cook, one of the great navigators of the era of exploration, went around discovering places that had always been there and then engaged in a bit of landscaping by planting the Union Jack, he and his crew couldn't really swim to any great efficiency and were particularly afraid of water.

Considering this, the accomplishments of those voyages and the courage it took to embark on them is pretty stark. And so were some of the swimmers that Cook and his crew came across. Starkers, in fact. The British were amazed at the way various Indigenous peoples fearlessly embraced the sea. They also noticed these same people either wore discreet 'sheaths' or nothing.

In the words of Sir Joseph Banks, the naturalist who contemporary judgement seems to position as the star attraction of the expedition while Cook was just the bloke who sailed the boat, the peoples they encountered didn't really scrub up in the swimwear stakes.

'Of all these people we had seen so distinctly through our glasses we had not been able to observe the least signs of Clothing: myself to the best of my judgement plainly discerned that the woman did not copy our mother Eve even in the fig leaf.'

It's not just some fruity piece of wit in his tome that chronicles that epic trek; his remark is loaded with an air of superiority, both racial and culturally, as he makes the point that not even Eve, the original Fallen Woman tempted by fruits of human pleasure, could come at being naked. She, at least, had a fig leaf.

And look, when you are left to the world of nature, you have to fight hard to be a little civilised – even Tarzan had to wear his loincloth. Spare me.

But old Joseph's comments just emphasise that the most fuss about swim attire is always about the female side, and most of the outrage, of course, has come from males.

Annette Kellerman was born near the end of the nineteenth century. She was a Mentone Grammar girl who lived a life and a half. She was a professional swimmer, vaudevillian, a silent film star and a vegetarian. I don't know what that has to do with anything but she thought it was important so we might as well give it a mention. She was at the forefront of the evolution of swimwear and popularised one-piece suits instead of women having to wear pantaloons.

'I can't swim wearing more stuff than you hang on a clothesline,' she said with good old Australian straightforwardness. But her stance came at a price; legend has it she was arrested at a public beach for indecency after complaints from male beachgoers.

It all blew over but in succeeding decades there was a litany of scenes on beaches where various middle-aged bullocks of men, Beach Inspectors – defenders of good taste and morality on the sands – measured swimwear, handed out fines and escorted women from the beach.

So, we come to the present-day land of cozzies, swimmers, togs and bathers – and who would have thought that there'd still be a chorus to ban what can be worn in public on a beach.

Every now and then it seems the temptation to tell people what they can and can't wear when they go for a swim proves a little too much to resist and the 'advice' is almost entirely directed at women. Sometimes it's the citing of one woman in a thong bikini near a beach that makes people turn into Joseph Banks muttering about Our Lady Eve and fig leaves. In fact, that's not a bad name for an association of swimwear pundits: The Old Banksian Society.

One Banksia Bloke, not that long ago, wrote to his local paper complaining about a woman who wore the tiniest triangle in front and was as close to naked as anyone could be from the back as she walked on a pavement near a beach.

He 'inadvertently' looked at the young woman in question who, it seemed, was almost challenging people to say something about what she was wearing. It made him feel uncomfortable and he also felt it was demeaning to women; it turned them into sex objects. And as problems with swimwear styles go, the old Inadvertent Banksian isn't alone. For in the summer of 2025, thong bikinis were banned at some municipal pools in Sydney, with Blue Mountains Leisure

Centres proclaiming that G-string thongs didn't fit the criteria as recognised swimwear.

It was all good for the exclamation mark people – be they mainstream media or influencers and social media types – to get hot and bothered and use lots of exclamation marks in covering the announcement.

There are dress codes everywhere when you think about it. You can't wear hats in RSLs, you have to wear a suit and tie in certain members' areas and standard lounge attire for men and women is requested at certain venues and functions.

So why can't the same apply to swimwear?

Well, that's the thing about the summer cozzie – it's like the season itself, sometimes way more is made of it than needs to be.

The first time I became fully aware of how what you wore to the beach could be eye-catching was one arvo as my parents, sister and I were all coming back from a swim at the beach.

It was late arvo or even early evening, for much of the heat had gone from the day, and my sister and I stopped at one of the red-brick beach shelters to lean against the wall. There you could leave a silhouette of your body, a watery shadow that you could watch slowly dry and evaporate before your eyes.

I remember my mother saying, 'And just like that it is gone. Was it ever really there?'

You could feel the heat of the day still in the bricks on your back and legs, almost a stinging sensation but not painful. And you would step off and look at the wet marks, the form of your body. And wait and stare as it disappeared, perhaps shaking off a bit more water from your body.

Was it ever really there?

I was shaking my legs waiting for the shadow to fade when I heard them. A family coming from the beach. Loud.

They had been splashing not far from us in the water and they had yelled and shouted to each other through the waves in a language I didn't understand. It sounded vaguely like some made-up dialect from a science fiction film. And now they were heading to the shelter, probably to leave their own watery shadows on the wall.

They came on as one – tumbling, rolling, jumping, tripping – like some great amorphous stop-motion animated creature, moving inexplicably forward with limbs extending and then retracting.

I heard my father say to my mother, 'Here comes the Yugoslavian Acrobatic Team.'

My mother of course said, 'Colin!'

I was too gormless to know if my father was joking. He was prone to a rather colourful alliteration when describing something that took his interest.

What particularly threw me about Dad's comment about the amorphous creature from the beach was the use of the term 'acrobatic team'. He had used that term when talking about the athletes who engaged in the gymnastic competition at the 1972 Olympic Games. 'Look at these acrobats, will you, full of muscles but couldn't throw a punch or kick a footy to save themselves.'

'Colin,' muttered my mother, 'they are called gymnasts.'

'Any coot who tumble-turns, does splits and stands on his head is an acrobat.' He had sounded very serious and certain and he used the same tone when he described the Yugoslavian Acrobatic Team on Suttons Beach.

They could be Yugoslavian, I thought. And acrobats. Lots of famous people visited Redcliffe. The Bee Gees had lived in Scarborough. Bobby Fulton, Artie Beetson, Graeme Langlands and the rest of the New South Wales state rugby league team had stayed at the Moreton Bay Hotel and some man called Acker Bilk, who played the clarinet and wore bowler hats, had relatives in Margate.

And apparently Bernard King had done a cooking demonstration in Walton's one all-day-shopping Saturday. So yes, these people could be what my father said they were.

As they neared the beach shelter, they smoothly disengaged from each other and fanned out almost in an arrowhead. For all the limbs and noise they made, they were only four separate human beings – and what a collection! They looked sort of awkward and odd-shaped but also rather strong, with broad chests and thick legs, and all built close to the ground.

What I was taken by, though, was what they wore. They all seemed to be wearing the same coloured togs, a grey beigey cream sort of hue. I say 'seemed' because it was also a little flesh-coloured and it was hard to decipher where the togs ended and the skin began.

The garments themselves were pulled up so high it was as if the wearers had attempted to defy gravity.

Years later in an art class where I had gained the exulted temporary position of life model, I gasped as I noticed a series of the Victorian-era English photographer Eadweard Muybridge's famous studies in the motion of the human body. Two men in rather doubtful-looking briefs in a variety of poses. They looked like the Yugoslavian acrobats.

All throughout that life class I stood starkers, save for a pair of slippers, and couldn't take my eyes off the photos. I could practically see the Yugoslavian acrobats standing around me.

Back near the beach that late arvo, the Yugoslav Muybridge life models came to a halt in their arrowhead formation and waited for us to vacate the brick wall. They stood with their arms bent at the elbows, the fingers on their hands all pointing towards their crotches. They seemed sort of suspended because their togs/bathers/cozzies/swimmers were pulled high to nose-bleed levels and it appeared as if they were hanging by the tops of their togs from a tree branch, the material straining upwards and sometimes outwards.

It reminded me of a cotton bag chockers with mangoes that a woman in Ella Street often hung off her clothesline. That bag had seemed as if it could burst at any moment.

'Oh, it's the Stranglers!' said my father in a friendly manner and he exchanged nods with the bullet-headed man.

My mother gave my father a look and then collected me and my sister after yet another hissed, 'Colin!'

We walked along for a bit and my sister broke the silence with, 'Why do they wear their togs like that, Mum?'

My mother held up a hand. When she spoke it sounded as if my sister had interrupted a ruminate in the front yard.

'No! It's their business,' she said curtly. Then she put one hand on the nape of my sister's neck and her other hand on my neck and said, rather ominously, 'But I can tell you, if ever you two wear anything like that in public, you'll be locked up.'

Being arrested for wearing togs – Annette Kellerman lives on!

Talk about doubling down. I didn't know what to think. But I worked out that even if the Stranglers were Slavic acrobats, they lived in Redcliffe. I saw them occasionally over the years. The father came around to hire some cement mixers from my father and on the blackboard that my father used to keep track of the deliveries for his hire business was the message, 'Electric Lightburn. To Stranglers.'

But whenever I saw or heard them around the traps, I couldn't get the swimming kit out of my mind's eye.

So when I saw Mr Stranglers in the Anzac Day parade, marching alongside my father and other returned men, all kitted out in their suits and ties, medals resting on their chests, I couldn't help myself. I still saw his medals — he'd earned them, I am sure — but I could only see him in those togs. And where he pinned the medals, well, that was his business.

The same with Mrs Stranglers when I saw her at the Country Women's Association stall at the Redcliffe Show, standing there among the sponges, lamingtons, tea urns and cupcakes. In her togs.

And once you started with the Stranglers, it sort of fuelled your imagination. I could picture all sorts of people wearing Stranglers Muybridge garments, from the postman on his bike, to Mr Clancy the round and incredibly pale Grade Four teacher at Humpybong Primary, to the butchers in their shops in Margate or Redcliffe — although I retained their knife scabbards because they looked sort of cool.

Sometimes it was the odd old lady waiting at a bus stop, the firemen next door, the occasional footy player — though never one of our Redcliffe Dolphins or any Brothers player (that didn't seem to be right). It was easy to imagine the refs and touch judges in their Stranglers Muybridge outfits, complete with piping whistles and little flags.

Even today the memory lingers.

One summer, years after I was introduced to the sight of the Stranglers in their flesh-coloured, gravity-inverted, mango-bursting bathers on the beach, I had a job at a supermarket.

My main purpose of employment was shelf-stacking, the odd trolley-collection mission and packing the paper bags with items purchased by customers. This last task I detested because I had no idea how to fill the bags properly, and no compunction to learn, so I was often faced with the doubtful looks of shoppers and the furrowed brow of the floor manager.

It got to the stage that, to escape too much attention, I would sometimes help a customer carry their shopping to the carpark.

One afternoon it was Mrs Stranglers. She nodded hello and said in heavily accented English, 'Young Mac'. I nodded back and carried her shopping to her car.

For some reason both my parents had a habit of popping into the shop when I was on shift. At the time I thought it happenstance but in hindsight I think they were most likely checking up on me and making sure I wasn't arsing about.

My mother had presented herself in the carpark at just this moment and exchanged a polite 'hello there' with Mrs Stranglers. Here, I thought, is a chance for me to add a bit of mayo and polish myself up a bit. I had packed all the bags, not letting the Stranglers woman touch a thing, and now carefully loaded them into the boot of her car, fussing a little bit for the benefit of my mother, making sure to demonstrate that I had done a thorough job.

I could see my mum was slightly surprised at my efficiency and dedication, so I thought I'd top it off with a hearty farewell.

'There you go, no worries at all, all safe and sound. Goodbye, Mrs Stranglers.'

She gave me a slightly odd look as she got into her car and when she shot a look to my mum I thought something might be up.

It was.

Mrs Stranglers' odd look was nothing compared to the one that greeted me when I turned to see how my mother had appreciated how well her youngest was going in the services industry.

Now, I was a large young lad, already playing the odd rugger game in the senior lower grades. But my mum, born and raised in the wilds of the Welsh mountains, was the sort of person who gave credence to the words of the Roman historian and politician Tacitus when he described the Welsh as a strong and warlike tribe.

Nobody can really ever express how much they love their mum – I know I couldn't – but I can definitely say old Tacitus was on the money. She looked strong and warlike as she poked me in the chest. 'You stupid boy!'

I had a feeling that all my dutiful work had been undone.

I just looked at her.

'What did you call her Mrs Stranglers for?'

'Isn't that her name?'

I felt as if I was a Roman legionnaire who was about to cop the pointy end of a rather sharp Celtic spear.

'You stupid boy, it's what your silly father calls them because of those atrocious togs they wore to the beach! And it's bad enough he calls them that!'

I couldn't help myself. 'She's not Yugoslavian then?'

Honestly, it's a wonder that the Romans got anywhere in Wales. The glare I got from my mother burnt two holes right through to the back of my head.

'Her name is Marjorie McDonald and she comes from Glasgow.'

That fact might explain my not understanding the accent.

Later that night, my father, obviously after being given a rocket by my mum, gave me a nod to join him in the front yard as he watered the garden.

I stood beside him as he kept his index finger over the end of the hose causing the water to squirt out in an uneven but rather lovely arc.

'Listen, boy, don't be using that sort of talk in public.'

'What talk?'

My father flicked the hose as he tried to hide his irritation. 'Oh Christ. The Stranglers talk. And calling Marj McDonald a Yugo.' He flicked the hose again and then had a think.

'Nothing wrong with Yugos of course, good tough people. But you know . . .'

He flicked the hose.

'What?' I asked. 'You called them Yugoslavian acrobats.'

'That was years ago.'

Hose flick.

Then a timeless piece of fatherly double-speak advice.

'Now listen, you. Doesn't matter what I said . . . but . . . you . . . you. You.'

He interspersed the you's with hose flicks. 'Don't you go bloody calling people things . . . even if they wear . . . bloody . . . togs from Dante's Fifth Ring of Hell.'

He flicked the hose as if it were a spitting snake he was trying to control.

Then he started laughing. 'The Stranglers. Yes, once seen, burns a scar in the memory.'

He tried not to laugh further, took a deep breath and then said sternly, 'Now listen, listen to me.'

I turned and faced him.

Then he pointed the hose square at me and drenched me while laughing and muttering about the Stranglers.

•

Swimwear is basically a collision between purpose and fashion. You don't really need high fashion statements when you go swimming, just something that is comfy to get wet, lets you move freely and is easy to dry. But humans, being humans, tend to make things more complicated than they need to be.

Jumping in water starkers is quite a lovely sensation, but there is a time and a place. Nude beaches, or naturist beaches if you want to sound as if you are broadcasting on Radio National, are quite plentiful.

As a drama student at the Western Australian Academy of Performing Arts I used to occasionally go to the Swanbourne nuddy beach in the 1980s with a lovely dancer who was studying at the same time as me. I told her that the idea of a nude beach didn't leave much to the imagination and might even ruin the idea of checking someone out on the beach.

She laughed a little.

'Checking out, huh?' she said. 'Is that what you call it?'

'Well,' I began and then stopped. What did I mean? Better not to say anything.

But my friend had a lovely smile on her face. 'Waiting!' she said. 'More please.'

'Well . . . you know.'

'Yes. Still waiting.' And her smile was still there.

'Well, everybody has a look at everybody, you don't have to stare, but you could look at somebody and quite like what you saw and maybe just keep it to yourself or maybe just have a bit of a chat with that person later on . . . maybe.'

She laughed. 'A bit of a chat after being checked out!'

I didn't know quite what to say but I told her I knew there was a difference between checking someone out and objectifying someone.

'I'm sure you do,' she said.

'Yes,' I said, 'it's not like gawping at someone.'

'Gawping?'

'Yes, you know, when you gawp at someone. You,' I paused and widened my eyes and tilted my head, 'gawp. You stare, that is gawping.'

She gave me a kiss, I remember.

And then she said, 'Good to know.'

She told me it was fun not to care too much about what you wore to the beach. She spent most of her week being taught how to meld her body this way and that, immersed in the discipline of ballet, being constantly aware of how she looked in the great walled mirrors of the academy's dance studios. She was taught to hold a leg just so and to extend her arms to a pinpoint in the air. She spent her time being checked out, if you like, by staff and other dancers, and checking herself out too.

So that is why she liked Swanbourne Beach.

She was right. After a while on that beach you didn't worry about what you and everybody else weren't wearing.

At uni a lecturer talked about the way 'Otherness' can affect people, how suspicious they become, how fearful of those who seem to be different and how that difference can be used to motivate, move and even control people.

But, really, we humans are a study in otherness. We are just as different as we are the same. And that point is certainly borne out on the sands of a nudist beach!

The bodies on display were almost like an exhibition of Lucian Freud's nude studies where the different shapes, sizes and folds of human flesh were celebrated.

Even so, there is a time and a place and we do like to complicate things.

There is always going to be some kind of 'Beach Inspector' who is likely to get worked up over what swimwear people might be wearing, or not wearing.

Remember, there always seem to be a horde of Old Banksians – both Inadvertent and Not – longing to give such advice and indeed in some cases take direct action. Like Old Banksian Hall of Famer Rex Mossop, a club-tongued dual rugby and league international who was a successful but polemic sports commentator from the seventies and eighties. Rex, who uttered tautologies as easily as he drew breath, made an out-of-season summertime 'citizens' arrest' of a nude bather in the late seventies.

Proudly boasting to the assembled exclamation-mark chasers – the media – Rex infamously said of his apprehension of the owner of the unclothed appendages, 'I don't want these people shoving their genitalia down my throat.'

A remark that he was quick to dine out on, excuse the pun, at sportsmen's lunches and speaking engagements. The irony is that, these days, only eight minutes drive from Rex's home is the rather aptly named Cobblers Beach, which has become one of Sydney's most popular naturist retreats.

If you frequent such a beach as Cobblers then you are in luck: no swimwear hassles and no Rex Mossop arrests.

The rest of us have to do what we can. But sooner or later doing what you can doesn't cut it. That's when you become aware of what you wear and how you look.

As a kid, it seemed to me that people used to wear the same swimwear for countless summers. Money wasn't something people would throw around on seasonal treats like bathing suits so you wore what you wore from the year before. I had a pair of red-checked shorts that I was squeezed into for what seemed like a decade. They became so tight it is a wonder I was able to sire children later in life.

My mother's swimming uniform was an industrial-strength blue one-piece bathing suit. It reminded me of the outfits weightlifters wore on the Sunday morning sports show *Sportscene*. They'd appear just after the trots segment, huffing and puffing, putting white powder on their hands and then clean-and-jerking all over the place.

The white powder was chalk to help with the competitors' grip but I always assumed it was talcum powder like my mum used – Johnson & Johnson or the more fancy Yardley.

Indeed, when you watched my mum about to enter the water, she was a little like the weightlifters before they would attempt to raise the great circles of steel. She would come to the water's edge, gather herself with a few deep breaths, then flick her hands the way they did before she girded her loins and got down to the task at hand; hers being to walk slowly into the waves.

Then she would gradually descend into the water and breaststroke about a bit before sighing and saying, 'How very lovely.' Afterwards, she would continue to swim and hum tunes to herself.

She would never put her head under the water and I never quite knew why the thought of submerging her nonce was so abhorrent to her, but I do know if you ever splashed near her or threatened to do so, you would get the Tacitus treatment and the howl of anger, 'No! No! No!'

Once when we were in the water waiting for my mum to go through her pre clean-and-jerk routine on the water's edge, I told my Old Man that I thought my mother's togs looked like the weightlifters' get-up.

My father looked at me, then at my mother, nodded and said, 'Bit of a stretch, Cabbagehead, but if you were half blind standing on your head and squinting, you might have a point.'

He floated for a bit, dove under and came up very close to me. 'Your mother is a strong woman all right. She'd give those fellas a run for their money.' And he winked.

He turned his head and looked at my mum again. 'She's a healthy lass all right and I'm a lucky man.'

Then he swam off towards her and laughed when she told him not to splash her.

3

BISCUIT BOX PEOPLE

Cricket and the tennis are often part of our summer background, which makes sense for not only are they both covered widely across the airwaves during the summer months, but cricket ovals and tennis courts dot our suburbs and regions. It is not uncommon to see a game of cricket being played while you go about your business. Usually the game consists of figures dressed in white standing around, often motionless. Nothing seems to be happening, but rest assured cricket is being played.

If I am in a car and I've stopped at an intersection or am waiting for the lights to change, I like to play a game of my own. I keep an eye on the cricket and the lights, and I wait for something to happen on the field, wait to see some indication of life taking place before the lights change.

And reassuringly, more often than not, absolutely nothing changes, except the lights. There is something almost ritualistic about the non-activity involved in our national summer activity.

Tennis has a similar appeal when it's just the punters playing on a suburban or regional court; when you catch a glance of someone reassuringly normal and ordinary trying to return serve or searching in the air for a lob. My own club is just up the road and I drove past recently, slowing down to navigate the roundabout. I could see a couple playing under floodlights, the moths diving in and out of the light, casting shadows on the blue court, the whole scene shimmering in a golden fluorescent glow. It struck me as being quite beautiful.

Cricket and tennis seemingly belong to the landscape of people; that's why they hold such sway over summer.

But yachting? It's one of the peculiarities of summer that the Sydney to Hobart is such an event. You don't even have to mention that it's a yacht race, because everybody knows it is, and that it starts on Boxing Day, and everybody knows it is an event. It's been going on since 1945 when what was supposed to be a cruise to Hobart became a race when an English yachtsman, Captain John Illingworth of the Royal Navy, who was serving at Garden Island (Illingworth RN sounds like the title character in a *Boy's Own Adventure Annual* story of derring-do, and he wasn't far from it) suggested at the end of an after-dinner speech that perhaps they ought to make a race of the cruise.

I like to think Captain Illingworth RN perhaps lounged on an elbow with a pipe in his mouth casually swirling an iced gin and tonic while he issued this polite wager, and that his Aussie hosts stopped mid-drink to consider, then pointed their half-full schooners at him and said, 'Too right, you're on.' Then downed their beers and thumped the empty schooner glasses on the bar.

In any case the rest, as they say, is history.

Yet the history of the race is never far from some competitors' minds. In 2015 Mark Richards, the skipper of *Wild Oats XI*, one of the modern maxi yachts that roar down the eastern coast to Hobart, said in an interview with the *Sydney Morning Herald*'s Rupert Guinness that he loves the race's history.

'The way it started is amazing . . . a bunch of guys, mates,' Richards said. 'That it has become an Australian icon is a big deal, and not just in Australia but worldwide.'

Although the main competitors, the glorious maxi yachts, are usually the playthings of international billionaires – even Ted Turner, the founder and one-time owner of CNN competed successfully in the race – the race's origins have that sense of Australian larrikinism in their DNA. So, while it may be a rich person's sport, the race belongs to everyone.

Back in 1945 the awful conflict of the Second World War had only finished a few months before that first Boxing Day start at twelve noon.

The world had torn itself apart and those competitors in the first race had been a part of that great awful upheaval, where they battled the forces of Militarism and Fascism. And what they had seen, what they had been a part of, one could hardly imagine now that peace had come. And how did they go about enjoying the peace?

A bunch of pals decided to sail down the eastern waters of Australia and risk their lives challenging the might of the open ocean, and they turned a life-threatening journey into a game, a bit of sport. Might as well have some fun if you're going to risk your life. That's what larrikins do.

It was a hardened generation finding a new test of adventure and proving themselves — just a bunch of blokes in woollen jumpers with big hearts and a bit of get-up-and-go. That endeavour is pretty easy to comprehend and the origins of the race — the idea of fronting up and having a crack at something, no matter how dangerous, because it might be a bit of a lark — are sentiments that almost all Australians would like to like to think reside in the national DNA.

Even today, competitors risk their boats, injury to themselves and sometimes their lives taking part in the race, and people who aren't remotely interested in sailing will observe with some pride how hazardous and harrowing the Sydney to

Hobart can be. The race's very nature, pitting oneself against the dangers of the open sea, instils a sense of national pride.

No wonder the thing took off. It's a bit like how the country went mad for the 1983 America's Cup win – an example of the ultimate humanising of Rich Guys' playthings – when Alan Bond, one of Australia's richest men at the time and an ace at creative bookkeeping, brought back the Auld Mug with his collection of Australian larrikins.

Somehow, we all won that cup, and even if it was a myth, it was fun and glorious.

I'm sure that some yacht clubs are fastidious private playrooms for Hooray Henrys, but I find there is something rather welcoming about yacht clubs in general.

There's a local yacht club or 'Yachtie' where I live and another one in the next village along. Yacht clubs and the sails of the boats dot the shoreline all along the area.

The clubs are a part of their communities and they always have something on that has nothing to do with sailing. Weddings, funerals, festivals, album launches, fundraisers and even old-fashioned cover bands and amateur DJs all find a home in the Yachtie.

One late summer's night not so long ago I wandered down the beach to the next yacht club along for an eighties night and found myself à la Billy Idol – that is, 'Dancing with Myself'. I was having a hoot and during what I thought was an energetic bit of late-middle-aged gyration to A-ha's 'Take

On Me' – a classic piece of Norwegian pop, based around the concept of English as a second language – I received a wonderful sledge-cum-praise from a fellow punter. A woman, who was pulling off a remarkable carry of five drinks and a packet of chips, stopped in front of me while I 'danced' and said, 'You're William McInnes, aren't you?'

I admitted I was, just at the same moment I thought that I might have been a bit too enthusiastic with the energetic thrusting and now felt slightly like Sir Toby of Hamstrung.

'You know,' said my gifted conveyer of drinks and potato chips, 'you dance the way Roger Moore skis in bad James Bond films.'

This I found rather funny and almost gave myself a stitch laughing, especially when I saw my reflection in the club's windows. I howled as I tried to replicate *The Spy Who Loved Me* or *For Your Eyes Only* and Roger in all his glory.

Actually, 'The Roger' sounds like a grand name for a novelty pop dance.

The Gifted Conveyer came back with a drink for me to make up for any offence that her remark might have caused, but I assured her being compared to Roger Moore had made my night and we toasted each other and then raised a glass to old Sir Roger.

•

I once started a Sydney to Hobart journey in the reference section of a Queensland university.

That's where I first met her. Or maybe she met me. She definitely saw me first, which is because I was pretty hard to miss. She was a student like me, only she had a part-time job in the library placing books back on the shelves after they had been returned then sorted. I was studying – in theory. I had completely cocked up my first year of tertiary education and was trying a novel approach to studying for my first-year final exams. I had recreationally enhanced to a rather meditative state and had decided to lie between two bookshelves where I could stretch either arm out to touch the spines of two books I should have been reading.

'Are you all right?' she asked.

With my eyes closed, I assured her that I was indeed fine.

'What are you doing?' She sounded mildly interested.

'I am studying.'

'Really?'

'By osmosis,' I explained.

She laughed. 'Like a frog, huh?'

I lay there, silent for a moment. A frog? The only thing I could think of was the story of the frog in the warm water that couldn't tell the heat was increasing. It ended up being boiled to death.

'You mean the boiling frog?'

'No. That's a parable, isn't it?'

A parable? If I'm learning about a parable, I thought to myself, maybe there is something to this frog study.

I was told by the voice that osmosis is the transfer of water through a membrane like a frog's skin and the solutes go from high to low in the process.

I was no solute expert, but I remembered the boiling frog. 'The boiling frog is a parable about the dangers of not noticing gradual change,' I said. 'Like in Germany in the 1920s, the Weimar Republic slowly gave ground to the National Socialists who evolved into the Nazis, and before the republic knew it, the waters had changed.'

'Very good,' she said.

'My lecturer told us that, I just remembered.'

'Really?'

'I added the bit about the waters changing. There is something to this frog stuff,' I declared.

She asked if I could move an arm so she could wheel the trolley through.

'I don't want to break the connection,' I said.

'Come on, Kermit.'

I rolled out of the way, and she rolled through.

'Good luck,' she said as she wheeled past.

'Thanks, but I think I'm going to end up like the frog.'

I stretched my arms back out and thought, I might as well ask.

'Will I see you again?'

'Maybe, Kermit. Maybe.'

I might be on here, I thought. She'd already given me a nickname, Kermit, the green frog from *The Muppet Show*.

Then I realised I hadn't opened my eyes. That meant I hadn't even seen her. So, I opened them but all I saw were the spines of books I should have been sifting through for knowledge. She and her trolley had moved on to the other aisle.

'Hey, what do you look like? How will I know you?'

'I'll find you, Kermit.'

And, miraculously, she did. At a party, after exams were out of the way. She came up to me and asked, 'How did you go in your finals, Kermit?'

I shook my head. No good. 'I blame you and your trolley for breaking my connection.'

She nodded and then smiled. 'I told you I'd find you.'

And I smiled back.

We had a lovely time together that summer. Nothing serious, really, but a lovely time that ended in a friendship.

I did get to meet her family, much to the delight of her father.

My friend had the reputation in her family of 'bringing home strays'; this referred to her 'menagerie of friends, acquaintances and occasional paramours', as my Aunty Rita would have put it.

We had bumped into my friend's brother at a pub and information was relayed back to her parents. This was at the height of me sporting a rather rogue mullet, which I think played a large part in how I was perceived. In fact, I'm pretty sure it played a definite part.

My friend's family home was in Brisbane and as I walked up the front steps of a rather lovely Queenslander, I heard what I assumed to be her father questioning her in a suitably father tone.

'This bloke you're going out with, is he the one Andrew was telling me about?'

I wondered what impression of me her brother Andrew had passed on.

'You know,' her father continued, 'the boofhead with the ape drape from Redcliffe?'

'Ape drape' was a rather colourful description of the mullet I had been offering to the world. I was happy to say that I had recently parted ways with it, but its effects had obviously lingered.

My friend said something in the affirmative and added, 'Andrew can talk!'

Andrew was a lovely bloke and I had little problem with his succinct character assessment of my good self. There was a pause and then her father said, 'Redcliffe! Does the bugger walk upright?'

My hometown did have a bit of a reputation in some of the 'better parts' of the state capital, but, again, I didn't take it personally and tried not to laugh as I knocked on the door.

My friend's father opened it and said, with a lovely smile and warm tone, 'Hello there, this must be William.' He extended his hand.

I couldn't help myself and stood bow-legged and beat my chest, hooted, and gave my best effort at a simian walk. I hooted again and then stood up, shook his hand and said hello.

He just stared, obviously embarrassed, but his daughter, wife and son fell about laughing.

'Fair cop,' he muttered, 'at least you've lost the mullet.'

We chatted a bit inside and when my friend and I were about to make our way out for the evening, he pulled me aside and muttered the threat cum quiet bit of advice that was popular for a while amongst certain types in the South-east Queensland Association of Fathers. It was purloined from the title of a supremely dreadful disaster film, about a volcanic eruption in the nineteenth century. 'Behave yourselves and get home at a reasonable hour or it's Krakatoa East of Java for you.'

'Oh, for goodness' sake, Eric,' was all his wife said.

I tried not to laugh.

They were a lovely family and they were fun — even the dad. He had that streak of friendly irascibility with a pinch of cantankerousness that seemed to be present in most middle-aged fathers of that time. He looked a little like Race Bannon, the bodyguard of Dr Benton Quest from the animated series *Jonny Quest*. The show was one of those cockamamie adventures that used to abound back in the day. It did, however, have a great theme tune with slangy twanging guitars that somehow morphed into some Dave Brubeck–inspired lounge jazz. And it had even better credits. Great lizards on leashes, pterodactyls, rather dubious interpretations of various indigenous peoples, mummies breaking through walls, flying saucers, fetching futuristic aircraft, two machine-gun-wielding frogmen being crushed by a speedboat, a great spider-like machine with a huge eye on a sphere with spindly legs and some sort of ray gun.

Dr Benton Quest was a widower with a suspiciously nervous look in his eye that suited his red-haired mo and goatee beard; in fact, he looked like a combination between a furtive and annoyed Gareth Evans – the Foreign Affairs minister and Attorney-General in the Hawke/Keating governments – and a shell-shocked biology teacher who'd lost control of a Year 10 class at high school.

Jonny was his son who, along with his dog, Bandit, and pal Hadji – an Indian boy wearing a turban complete with a massive jewel in the front – would get up to all sorts of adventures battling low-rent though delightfully drawn bad guys.

Benton Quest was an inventor, vaguely associated with the fight for freedom and upholding the American way. In truth, he was a nerdy plot device for Race Bannon, my pal's dad's look-alike, to do his gung-ho bodyguard stuff.

Race Bannon had short white hair, seemed very sure of himself and was an action man. These were true of both Race and my pal's dad, though while Race battled baddies, my pal's dad was in a constant state of movement and action – and they both ran like their legs were too short for them and pumped their arms like pistons.

Race's run I put down to the way he'd been drawn and animated; my pal's dad's run, I suppose, was down to how his gene pool worked. It didn't seem to slow him down, though. His crouched rocket run and pumping arms seemed like a tribute to the movie star Tom Cruise and his over-produced action hero run.

And through the years, on the odd occasion I happened to be watching a Tom Cruise action flick, whenever the tiny superstar would break into a sprint I thought rather fondly of Race Bannon/my pal's dad.

But there was something else that the whole family made me think of and even in their company I could never quite put my finger on what they reminded me of.

They were happy, sporty, had a subscription to the Royal Queensland Theatre Company, were relatively affluent, and well dressed.

I had never known a family to wear clothes that always seemed to fit. Even when the father wore business shorts, long socks (with a pen tucked in on the inside of an immaculately turned-down sock hem), a short-sleeved business shirt (more pens in the breast pocket) and a tie pinned at the third button, he seemed to pull it off.

He was a bit of a yachtsman and kept a small craft. He often crewed larger boats too. They were certainly an active lot and he and the rest of his brood loved to play tennis, board games – especially a game called Yahtzee, perhaps because during the game someone got to yell out the game's name at the top of their lungs – and word puzzles.

The father liked me a little more when he realised I wasn't a long-term prospect for his daughter and had become simply a mate. That and perhaps my comment when I overheard him at a barbecue talking about a yacht called *Helsal*.

I added, 'The old Flying Footpath.'

He looked at me in a rather surprised way and said, 'You know *Helsal*?'

I said I did: the ferro boat that Tony Fisher won the Brisbane to Gladstone in.

He stared.

'They called it the Flying Footpath,' I continued, 'because it was covered in ferro cement.'

'I know that,' he almost snapped. 'But how do you know that, Simian?'

I could have told him that I had always remembered a McCrae cartoon from the 1976 *Courier-Mail* about the winner of that year's Brisbane to Gladstone, the yacht *Helsal*. I also remembered some of the older members at the Humpybong Yacht Club banging on about it when myself and a few schoolmates were mucking about in single-handers like the little one-man Laser sailing boats under their tutelage. *Helsal* had won the 1973 Sydney to Hobart, so the fact it was competing in the local blue ribbon sailing event made it a bit of a talking point.

I had heard from a friend who was a yachtie that the poor old Flying Footpath, which had been sold as a day cruiser to somebody in the Philippines just three years after the 1976 Gladstone win, had sunk during a cyclone.

I think this was the subject of the barbie chat. I heard my friend's father say, 'What a shame to see an open sea racer like *Helsal* end up like that.'

But I didn't think he needed to know all that background; it was time for a bit of fun. I added a bit of mayo to those few months I'd spent at Woody Point mucking about at the yacht club in little single-handers.

'People sail on the Redcliffe Peninsula, you know,' I said, 'at the Humpybong Yacht Club.'

'Oh,' somebody cooed, 'dear old Humpybong Yachtie! I love that name.'

My friend's father looked at me. 'You're an old salt, Simian,' he said, rather sceptically.

'Simian?' the partner of the woman who had cooed over the quaintness of Humpybong asked. 'Is that an Irish name?'

I tried to think of something to say to that but my pal's father piped up, 'Yes. Yes, it is. Gaelic for sea-going ape, isn't it, Simmy?' And he winked.

'Oh, really?' cooed the woman again.

I nodded.

My friend's father almost smiled then said, 'You want another beer?'

I didn't really see much of my friend's family after that because I ended up continuing my journey through tertiary education at another uni after failing spectacularly and unsurprisingly at my first attempt. After finishing that degree, I went off to drama school. But we managed to catch up occasionally, which was always rather fun due to the competing nicknames they had bestowed on me.

'Kermit is just down from Rocky, and we popped over to say hello,' my friend would say.

'Oh, hello, William,' her mum would reply.

'You been behaving yourself, you Redcliffe Simian?' her father would say as he shook my hand.

After my first year at WAAPA I came home in the summer break. And it was during that break that I finally worked out what my pal's family reminded me of.

Biscuit Box People.

In our home we followed certain festive traditions of a singular nature. The Christmas tree was always chosen from one of the branches of the pine tree in the front yard and was given a name, so that it almost became a member of the family at Christmas.

One branch was called Dino because no matter how much you tried to straighten it in the bucket it always slouched over to one side, almost as if it were sloshed. A little like Dean Martin during his television show.

Our house's windows would be covered in festive decorations painted on with sandshoe whitener, a substance that was used to paint over grimy sports shoes or runners. These were the days before Bunnings or some other retailer made copious amounts of generic household decorations to stick in windows or in the front yard, just so your home could look like the place next door.

Another family tradition was the biscuit box. Most festive biscuit boxes were made of tin and had odd children with light-coloured eyes and red or straw-coloured hair. They usually sat with forced smiles and some nervous sad-eyed dog like a spaniel or a corgi. They were quite frankly disturbing, as if they were cousins of the kids from the *Village of the Damned*. And the biscuits were nearly always shortbread and had an otherworldly taste that seemed to suit the image on the lid.

The other biscuit box favourite was a ballet scene or, as one of my sisters said, 'a ballerina dancing scene', usually from *The Nutcracker* or some other Tchaikovsky work.

But Queensland always had a character unique unto itself and in Brisbane there had been a bakery called Webster's that used to be in the suburb of Dutton Park. It was a family-owned business that thrived for decades until it was eventually bought by the bigger Australian company of Weston's, and the production was moved to a larger factory in Chermside.

The Webster's name was kept for the Queensland customers who had grown used to enjoying a homegrown product. The biscuits were okay as mass-produced biscuits go, but one thing that was unique about the company was their Picnic Pack. It was a large square box filled to the brim with a variety of different bickies. A banner on one of the side panels assured whoever was about to lift the lid and delve into the contents that they could rest easy with what they would pull out because, the panel claimed, 'This pack contains the Finest Variety of Cream Filled and Sweet Biscuits ever packed'. There was no exclamation mark – it was as if it were a statement of undeniable truth, although the important words were given capitals to make sure we knew something worthwhile awaited us in the box.

And the images. Bizarrely utopian, almost like a propaganda poster from some totalitarian state. Each panel depicted a different activity and illustrated how your enjoyment could be accentuated by the finest bickies ever packed.

On the top was a picture of a family picnic – which makes sense, the thing was called the Picnic Pack after all – showing a mother with shining earrings the size of golf balls, a waist as neat as an hourglass, fetching short brunette coiled hair, a high-collared plunging blouse and a hint of the outdoors with perhaps denim tapered slacks. Not jeans, but denim 'slacks', if there was ever such a thing.

Behind her were two children dressed in clothes for running around: the boy shirtless in shorts; the girl in a sleeveless short pantsuit get-up. They sat above an opened Picnic Pack staring down like pirates who have found a treasure chest, but also like innocents, almost in an act of supplication.

The father sat on a nearby log with his head to one side, a cup of most likely tea in his hand, almost as if he was on a smoko and was pondering the scene before him.

The mother was holding out yet more biscuits on a proffered plate, smiling with a band of gleaming teeth.

Our family's Picnic Pack was probably bought not long before or after I was born. Long after the finest bickies ever packed had been gobbled up, the box was kept as a decorative container for more biscuits and treats bought over the succeeding Christmases. Even though it was a Webster's, all sorts of manufacturers' efforts went into the Picnic Pack: Arnott's, Weston's, Walker's Shortbread, Nabisco, Peek Freans, ginger snaps, Brockhoff's. Almost anything could be expected to appear in that box at Christmas, from homemade

Anzac biscuits that looked like a relief map of the Great Dividing Range but tasted wonderful, to Arnott's Teddy Bears and the highly dubious Golliwog chocolate-flavoured biscuits – the look on the faces of these biscuits. The Picnic Pack was like a king's treasure chest full of bounty from the Biscuit Barons.

One Christmas, when the box was beginning to look a bit worse for wear, it was filled to the brim with Allen's Snakes. It could have been a scene from an Indiana Jones movie: the bold adventurer reaching into a chest of archaeological prizes only to find a writhing mass of his least-liked living thing.

Instead of saying, in a suitably Harrison Ford growling baritone, 'I hate snakes,' it probably should have been, 'I ate snakes.'

The snakes seemed slightly at odds with the box's purpose, but my mother brushed that idea off by saying that she hadn't had the time to find biscuits and thought snakes would do, 'As the things are quite colourful in a Christmas way, very decorative.'

When she was asked what snakes had to do with Christmas, she replied as if she were talking to an idiot, 'Oh, for good-ness' sake, there's always snakes somewhere in the Bible – why couldn't they be in the manger?' Then she pointed to the biscuit box. 'There'd be one around that picnic! Look at the bushland in the back. We all know what that means. Eastern brown, most likely.'

It was my mother and father who alerted me, as they had done with all their children, in their wonderful tongue-in-cheek way, as to how the scene on the box had the look of a nativity setting. The biscuits were the centre point and took the place of the newborn king. When I looked a bit lost my father helpfully guided me, 'Come on, boy, why do you think they give you a bickie at Communion? Eh?' and he winked.

And my mother said, 'Oh Colin.'

The father on the log was Saint Joseph. 'Poor old Joe, trying to figure out what was going on. He could come at the first one, then maybe the second, but the third one?' My father was talking about the two children already there, staring down at the Picnic Pack.

'How many immaculate conceptions could you have?'

'Colin!' my mother said, louder, and she started laughing.

And the mother on the box? Well, she was just offering the good biscuits that she'd already put aside for the Three Wise Men. Iced VoVo, Monte Carlo and Chocolate Ripple.

Only polite if you are receiving gold, frankincense and myrrh.

My mother, perhaps thinking that I might have been a tad gormless, thought it best to point out that it was just a bit of fun.

'You have your faith, but you can also have a bit of fun with it. We are lucky because we live in a home where that's allowed.'

By home she didn't just mean the battleaxe block in Redcliffe, I think she meant Australia, which in retrospect is lovely.

My father added, not for the first time, 'Just remember not to take it too seriously, but know who to ride with when things might be bumpy. That coot Jesus – he's a good 'un.'

My mother would look at the mother on the Picnic Pack and say, 'Oh, look at her, all dressed up and that tiny waist! If she's given birth to two children, then I'm the Queen of Tonga on a pogo stick.'

The rest of the panels got a similar treatment. They were all versions of what my mother called 'Biscuit Box People' – where clothes fit, nobody is grubby or dirty or fat, and people are all smiling those white smiles as if they are wearing brand-new mouthguards.

The side panels had a different feel to the top of the box. They were like frescos or murals and the figures had an almost genderless quality about them; the forms smooth with elongated limbs and oversized heads. The biscuit people at the beach and playing tennis didn't look like they had exerted themselves and, save for a tight and neatly pressed style on their head, were otherwise hairless. They didn't sweat, didn't get wet, didn't strain and yet they were happy in a gleaming mouthguarded-smiling way. The overall feel was slightly surreal and yet pretty basic in its meaning: Queensland families accentuating the glories of living in the form of playing tennis,

72

being at the beach, celebrating life at a birthday and, of course, watching television.

Biscuit Box People.

My mother once told me, as I tucked into a collection of biscuits and party mix lollies from the Picnic Pack box one Christmas, that nobody, really, is a Biscuit Box Person.

She was quite fond of saying little poems and sometimes at night when we were much younger she'd tuck us into bed with these words:

Nighty night and sweetly rest
Like the birdy in its nest
For this is where the little elves
Cuddle down to hide themselves
Into fluffy beds they creep
Close their eyes
And go to sleep.

If you stayed up and mucked around, she'd boom out, 'Go to bed or I'll send in the goblins to get you!'

She had another little poem she'd say occasionally, and I never knew whether she'd made it up herself or she had been taught it as a child. It was this poem she recited as I tucked into the contents of the Picnic Pack box one Christmas and I think it was meant to let us know that there was a commonality to the idea of being a human being.

That nobody was ever really a Biscuit Box Person.

'We're all in the same boat, remember; you've got to understand that people are people, no matter what they may have.' And then she'd say the poem.

We live and breathe and laugh and cry
And learn and love and struggle and try
And win and lose and then we die
And at the end when it's time for goodbye
If hearts are full of love that will tell
Of a happy soul and a life lived well.

And then she would nearly always nod and say, 'There you are!' and tap you gently on the head.

That first incarnation of Biscuit Box People didn't end well. Over the years it had served us stoically, but aside from the wear and tear of being the receptacle of festive treats over that time it had been adorned with additions to the illustrations on the box. Oddly, nobody touched the nativity-based effort on the top, but the side panels were fair game.

So, to the happy Biscuit Box People were added various eye patches, tattoos, sunglasses, cigarettes in mouths, and even a spear in the back of one of the Biscuit Box Beach People and a tomahawk in the head of one of their smiling Biscuit Box Tennis cousins.

It was as if we children were trying to take down the Biscuit Box People a bit, make them a little less perfect, but once you start on that road you are led to rack and ruin.

I sealed the box's fate when, on one long-ago arvo, I grabbed a darning needle and made holes in the Biscuit Box People then pushed through plasticine, creating a three-dimensional aspect to the proceedings.

My mother wasn't happy. 'Oh, you've ruined it now! You stupid boy, the eye patches and the hatchets were one thing but what have you done?'

She said this in a rather accusatory tone while holding out the box with the little pipes of plasticine poking through. 'What is this supposed to be?'

I didn't really know what I thought they were, but I came up with, 'They've got worms?'

'Worms? He looks like he's doing goggers!' She was pointing to the tennis-playing Biscuit Person – the one without the tomahawk in his head. 'Goggers' was my mother's term for defecating, a word she'd brought with her to Australia from her home in Wales. I don't know if it was a Welsh term, although I tend to think not; it was for some reason simply a word created in the home she grew up in and brought to the other side of the world.

Somehow goggers was supposed to sound more polite than poo or any of the other words used to describe this bodily function.

'Well, we can't use this anymore, nobody wants to have Christmas snakes and bickies from a box covered in Biscuit People with worms and doing goggers!'

And that was the end of that Picnic Pack. It disappeared under the stairs, a halfway place for items destined for the bin. Its place was taken by a pristine edition of the Picnic Pack from the early seventies that had been kept in reserve by my mother until the old Biscuit Box People were retired.

The weight on this box was indicated in metric instead of the old imperial measurements, but the template of the box of treasures was the same: nativity picnic on top; tennis, beach and lounging in front of the television on the side. But this time the illustrator who had done the side panels had also done the nativity scene on top and the feel was slightly different.

Old Saint Joseph/Dad looked quite happy on the log and the kids wore clothes and didn't really appear like they were kneeling before a deity. The mum didn't look like she was so at odds with reality this time. No golf ball earrings, just a normal outfit. Neat and perfectly fitted of course, but the feel was different. My aunty said it was like, 'The Good News version of the Bible, where they've tried to make everything very conversational, like some odd person is talking to you while you are waiting at the bus stop.'

My mother looked at the box and thought for a while then agreed, 'Yes, very Vatican Two, isn't it?'

Then they laughed.

The Picnic Pack soon stopped being brought out at Christmas and instead sat on a shelf, filled with decks of various cards. The figures on it were still called Biscuit Box People and the cards became the new treasures within, which seemed quite apt. And a little family tradition passed into family folklore.

•

That first Christmas and New Year break back from drama school I was sitting at the table while my mother and her sister played gin rummy. I grabbed a deck of cards from the Picnic Pack for a game of Patience. I used to like to sit and play and listen to them chat together, gossiping, telling old stories, roaring with laughter about old farmers they had known or commenting on how odd the new butcher at Clontarf was. Sometimes they would sing together while they played. Songs from their childhood in Wales, songs from the radio – just songs.

I still play Patience today and when I do, as I sit alone, somehow I can still hear them and their lovely old tunes and it makes me happy.

But on that day, they were chatting about the newish Lord Mayor of Brisbane, Sallyanne Atkinson, the first woman and the first Liberal to hold the position. She wasn't your usual public official, having been born in Sydney, raised in Colombo and then on the Gold Coast, before becoming a journalist and then marrying a neurosurgeon from Brisbane. They had travelled to Europe and now, as well as raising a family, Sallyanne had found time to become lord mayor.

She had made quite a splash because she was a new type of politician. She was a woman and she was well educated. The fact that she was a Liberal was a novelty, but that wasn't the thing that mattered.

It was the way she looked and sounded.

'Marj McDonald says she wasn't born in Brisbane, that's why she sounds the way she does, hoity toity,' said my aunt.

'Hoity toity! Marjorie McDonald was born in Glasgow and I can't understand a word she says, at least I can understand Sallyanne Atkinson,' said my mother.

'How is the old Yugoslavian acrobat going?' I asked. That family in their odd togs long summers ago had haunted my mind.

'Stupid boy,' was all my mother said.

My father joined in from around the corner where he sat in 'his' chair. 'Oh, she's all right for a Tory, at least she's up and about and having a crack.' Probably some of the highest praise my father, a Labor man, could offer.

Sallyanne Atkinson was indeed having a crack and was one of a series of lord mayors, starting with Clem Jones, going on through Frank Sleeman to Roy Harvey and Sallyanne herself who helped transform Brisbane into the modern city it has become. She shepherded the old town through Expo 88, which was looming just the year after next.

'I always thought that she looked a little like the Biscuit Box Mother, the old Picnic Pack Mother, you know the one with the light bulbs for earrings,' said my own mother.

Golf balls to some and light bulbs to another, but I knew exactly what she was talking about. I stood with my hands on the lid of the 'new' Picnic Pack on the shelf and looked at the top of the box after closing the lid.

No, the mother on the new Picnic Pack didn't look like the lord mayor, but the old one did.

And suddenly I realised who the woman on the box did resemble and what my friend's family in the nice Queenslander in the nice suburb in Brisbane reminded me of – Biscuit Box People.

The parents even looked like the parents on the bloody thing, and the side panels could almost have been renderings of their love of all things recreational: swimming, tennis and games.

I laughed.

My mother asked why I was laughing like that.

'Like what?' I asked.

'Like you're laughing at somebody. I know that laugh.'

I told her that the Biscuit Box People reminded me of someone too.

'Now listen, you, I didn't say Sallyanne Atkinson was a Biscuit Box Person, I said she looked like one. There's a difference – you just remember people are people, nobody has everything.'

I nodded.

•

Later that week I walked up the steps of my pal's nice family home and I smiled.

Biscuit Box House.

I was greeted by the mother who was, as I could have imagined, dressed for tennis. She told me my pal had been kept busy back at her part-time job at a café in Brisbane, but she wouldn't be long.

An Engelbert Humperdinck song was playing rather loudly and was echoing down a hall that led to the kitchen.

My pal's mum told me to come in and, 'Plop yourself down in the living room. Eric's just watching the television and I'm rustling up a snack. Would you like something?'

I told her I would thank you very much and a part of me hoped it might include biscuits in a Picnic Pack. Before I could ask if she'd like a hand she added, 'He's in a bit of a funk, slipped over and did his ankle crewing for someone at the club. You go and say hello.'

The father sat in a chair, his left foot bandaged at the ankle and propped up on an ottoman. He looked like a very sad sorry Race Bannon indeed.

'Simian,' he said a little morosely in welcome.

'What did you do to yourself?' I asked.

He just shook his head. I noticed that, even though he was obviously incapacitated, he looked immaculate in casual wear.

The television screen was showing what I took to be Sydney Harbour. White sails filled the screen, looking like some primary school class's attempts at origami – lots of white triangles of different sizes scattered everywhere.

I thought there was either a break in transmission or the image was a graphic of some kind because nothing seemed to be happening.

The Engelbert Humperdinck song also seemed to be going on a long time.

The television remained frozen. Engelbert kept singing. Nobody spoke.

I realised the song was playing over again after a few minutes. It was called 'Too Beautiful to Last'.

Engelbert Humperdinck wasn't the singer's real name; he had borrowed his name from a well-regarded nineteenth-century German composer. The fellow singing the song was a tall, good-looking fellow in a rubbery, heavily tanned, big-toothed sort of way. I remember my mother saying she didn't like the way he wore his dinner suit on his TV show, 'The boy looks like he hasn't any crotch. He's a big doll, lovely voice though.' He sang love songs mostly, plaintive ballads to syrupy lounge orchestrations. This one was no exception.

It was about how all who love are doomed to die just like winter roses, how dreams and love that are shared and dared fade away into the shadows of the past. Too beautiful to last.

It was a pretty song but hearing it for the fourth time was slightly unsettling.

I tried a conversational gambit, 'Fond of this song?'

The father shook his head, not taking his eyes off the television and pointed off to the left. 'She is.' He meant his wife.

After a moment, he explained that his wife was fond of making tapes of songs she liked, and that when she liked a song she liked to hear it over and over again.

Her usual number of replays was five.

He said five, elongating the word, I think to demonstrate how long he had been listening. He half smiled when I tried not to laugh. Then he took a deep breath and said, 'Sorry, Simian, I'm in a bit of a trough.'

He was silent and then as Engelbert finished and began again, he spoke. He said he'd been expecting a promotion at his work that would see him out. But somebody else got it. A young bloke. A good bloke. Just younger. He hadn't told anybody until after he'd done his ankle.

He'd come home, angry. Not at anyone in particular, just angry. He wouldn't be going anywhere further in his job; he'd finish where he was.

He'd gone out to crew a yacht in a big swell. He knew it was too tough for what he could manage, but he wanted to prove he could still do it.

He couldn't. He was awkward and unsteady. A few years earlier he would have been fine, but he was just a bit of a fossil now. He'd tripped and done his ankle. They'd brought the boat back and nobody had said anything.

'I think they were trying to be nice about it.' He sighed.

He'd been laid up for a week and his wife was looking after him. He smiled. 'That's why she put the Sydney to Hobart on, it's a tape of the start of this year's race. She thought I might like it.'

I asked him when it was going to start or if he had paused it.

He smiled again. 'It's been going for about fifteen minutes. I turned the sound down because the people covering it are just talking drivel.' He turned to me and said, 'I preferred two efforts of Shirley Bassey screaming her lungs out and four Engelberts whining away.'

We both laughed.

'It is really odd to see something you love doing,' he pointed a finger at the screen, indicating the yachts, 'come across as so bloody dull and boring. Like watching paint dry.'

I waited a moment and offered, 'It's all a matter of perspective.'

He didn't say anything for a bit. Maybe he thought I was trying to be smart, but I wasn't. Finally he said, 'You might be right but it's still bloody boring.'

Engelbert warbled away again. 'What's on after old Humperdinck Pumpernickel?' I asked.

He shook his head again. 'You don't want to know.'

We stared at the Sydney to Hobart. Nothing was happening.

I got up and said I'd see if I could be useful in the kitchen. He nodded. Engelbert warbled and I walked down the hall, following the noise of the crooning. He was getting through to the end, before he fired up for the last time.

I turned in to the kitchen and there I saw my friend's mother, in her tennis kit, a white headscarf just like that worn by the Biscuit Box Mother on the panel where the Biscuit Box People go to the beach. She was mixing spoons of Keen's mustard powder in a small silver server that she was about to place on a tray of what I thought were ham and cheese sandwiches. She was also talking to herself. About what I didn't know. I couldn't hear because Engelbert was singing.

I didn't know quite what to do. People talking to themselves never bothered me, I mean half of Redcliffe did that. My dad would give speeches he never got to give in parliament to our dogs as he painted his trestles and when I overheard them, I just let him carry on. In truth, they were pretty good speeches and the dogs seemed to enjoy them, tilting their heads this way and that.

Better to step back out of the kitchen and call out a hello and re-enter, giving fair warning. As I stepped back, Engelbert stopped and as the mother furiously and efficiently whisked the mustard powder into paste, I heard what she was saying.

'Well, Sallyanne, we have to get everybody working together: business, the unions and the people, to make Expo work. We can do it.'

I didn't laugh, although seeing someone in a tennis dress with fetching red piping, white headscarf, white socks and tennis shoes furiously agitating a silver spoon in a small silver serving dish to mix mustard powder and pretending to talk to the Lord Mayor of Brisbane about Expo 88 was more than enough reason to laugh.

I stepped back and gave a loud 'Hello!' before I came back into the kitchen. I could tell by her face that she was a little embarrassed, but after a second she seemed content that I hadn't heard her sage advice to Sallyanne Atkinson.

I asked if I could help and she said, 'Oh, that's nice of you,' and told me to take two glasses and two cans of light beer into the living room, she'd just finish up the ham sandwiches.

Engelbert warmed up again and I headed back to the frozen Sydney to Hobart race on the big Rank Arena television set.

I gave the father a glass and the can of light beer, he nodded a thankyou and looked at me. He said that he thought I was going off to do law down in Sydney the last time I saw him and I told him that was the plan, but it had sort of got interrupted.

By what?

'Not wanting to do law. I don't know, I deferred a year to see how the acting thing went.'

'And how'd it go?' he asked.

'Well enough to stick it out,' I said.

What sort of acting did I like? he asked.

I just looked back at him.

'I mean, do you like movies?'

I nodded that I did. I couldn't work out whether he was bored with the Sydney to Hobart or trying to be polite and make conversation. Or perhaps he was genuinely interested.

'What's your favourite movie, Simian?'

I was going to say *Dr Strangelove*, but I couldn't help myself.

'*Planet of the Apes*, I reckon,' I told him.

He said that was a beauty. 'That bit at the end when Charlton Heston sees the broken Statue of Liberty and just screams because he realises that we buggered everything up. Terrible, that moment you've worked out that you've buggered up something.'

He sat very still, took a deep breath and nodded his head. 'Yeah, I liked that movie. Got any others?'

This was odd, why so many questions? '*Beyond the Planet of the Apes . . . Beneath the Planet of the Apes*, they were good.'

He raised his eyebrows. 'You like science fiction, huh? Anything else?'

I told him that I had a soft spot for the Clint Eastwood film *Every Which Way but Loose*.

'The one with the monkey?' He nodded. 'You like Clint? He's a beauty, love *Dirty Harry*.'

'He's okay,' I said, 'but I really liked the monkey.'

He stared at me.

'The orangutan. Terrific performer.'

And he burst out laughing. He laughed so much his bad foot moved slightly on the ottoman, and he winced. I went to ask him if he was okay and he held up a hand.

'All right,' he said. 'I suppose you like *King Kong*?'

'Oh yes, fine simian cinema.'

'Of course. And *Tarzan* you'd be –'

I didn't let him finish.

'Cheetah, champ chimp actor.'

He smiled, half laughed and then told me he had always admired Bonzo, another monkey actor from *Bedtime for Bonzo* in which the chimp co-starred with an actor by the name of Ronald Reagan, who was at that time the current President of the United States. I assured him I would have voted for Bonzo.

'Goes without saying,' he said. Then he laughed quietly and said almost affectionately, 'Smart-arse.'

He stared at the television again while Engelbert was crooning about rainbows. My pal's dad said he liked going to the theatre but wasn't sure how you'd go about earning a living as an actor. What did my parents think?

I told him they'd wondered that too. I paused. And then I told him how my father had rung me up in Perth, out of the blue, to ask how I was going.

'Oh, yes?'

I nodded. 'My Old Man just rang up the academy one day and asked to speak to me. I got called out of a class because he said he needed to talk to me. I went to the office and picked up the phone and he asked how I was. He must have been ringing up from a public phone, the one down by the beach at Scarborough. Maybe the Old Man had been delivering trestles and suddenly thought he'd give me a bell. I could hear seagulls and waves. I could hear home. Maybe, I thought, he just decided to ring, grabbed a handful of silver from the glove box or the ashtray of his truck and fed them into the phone and called me. He's waited for me to come, maybe he was running out of coin for he sounded – not impatient – but as if he wanted to get to the point. He said, "Are you happy?" And "Do you think you can make a go of it?"'

'And you said?'

'I said I was happy, that it was like a team sport, and I might be able to make a go of it.'

My friend's father asked me what my dad had said.

This was a strange conversation. No grown-up had ever really shown an interest in what I was doing and here was this Biscuit Box Dad with his foot bandaged and banged up before a frozen yacht race of origami cast-offs talking to me about my life.

I thought I might as well tell him what my father had said.

'My Old Man told me that he had my back. He told me I was his boy and to get stuck in. And . . . he told me he loved me.'

There was a silence filled by Engelbert finishing off that interminable bloody tune.

I wasn't used to being this honest talking about myself and I found it very hard not to cry.

The father held his can of light beer like Yorick's skull and then said, 'Your dad said that? He sounds like a good man.'

I managed to say he was.

He still Yorick-ed with the can of beer, then he looked me straight in the eyes and said, 'Brace yourself for what's about to hit.'

If we were at sea I'd be expecting an iceberg. Instead it was something else.

'Here's your ham sandwiches!' said his wife, appearing in her immaculate tennis apparel. She put the plates down on the small table that stood between the chairs we sat on and placed the little silver mustard dish delicately in the space between the plates. She said she was off to freshen up, and as she left the next song began.

'Ob-La-Di, Ob-La-Da', a Beatles song by Paul McCartney, only it wasn't the Beatles singing it.

Now, music can mean many things to many people, and I am certainly no judge of quality, but as the saying goes, you know what you like, and you know what you don't. During that first year at WAAPA we were introduced to different streams of the arts – from choral work to jazz to musical theatre and basic singing – and of all the forms that were traversed, I can honestly say that a cappella, the form of singing where the singer or singers perform a song with no musical accompaniment, was the most annoying.

As a pal of mine, Sahara, put it as we headed into a class, 'Here we go, more of this "Hey Nonny, Nonny" bullshit.'

I couldn't have agreed more. The idea of singing along with voices only is fun when you think of people spontaneously singing a footy club song, or something else binding and communal. Another English a cappella group, The Flying Pickets, did a cracking version of the Alison Moyet song 'Only You'.

But people, being people, just don't know when to stop and they have to fart around and add silly noises, 'pop' sounds, grunting and any idiotic aural rubbish to prove how marvellous an instrument the voice can be.

Enter The King's Singers. An a cappella group from England who took their name from King's College, Cambridge, where they were all studying music – yes, musical scholars, brains as big as planets probably, and tonsils full of silly noise.

To some they are creative, spontaneous and tuneful but to the likes of me they were twitty, toffy-looking pommy twinks, with odd English faces. The sounds they emitted were like a prehistoric synth, almost achieving the unique transition of the human voice into an electronic novelty.

They were probably nowhere near that bad, but they haunted programs like the Cleo Laine Show and Nana Mouskouri Show on Friday nights on the ABC, which were adored by people, especially mothers, in places like Brisbane's 'better' suburbs. The King's Singers were a favourite because they were so well-spoken and cultured.

The old King's boys managed to turn McCartney's great ode to working-class family life into the aural version of high tea with cucumber sandwiches, Pimm's and Earl Grey chasers.

The Sydney to Hobart had never had such a soundtrack to its endeavours.

My friend's father was, I am pretty sure, on the same wavelength. He sat with his eyes closed while he slowly raised his arms then tightly balled his fists and stretched his mouth and face into a grimace that could have put Munch's *The Scream* to shame. Then he took a breath and said, in a seething whisper, 'I cannot fucking abide the fucking King's FUCKING SINGERS.'

He sat with his eyes closed for a moment and then said, 'But she likes them, so fair enough.'

I assumed 'she' was his wife.

'Oh,' I said. 'One of the boats has broken away, it's moving!'

He opened his eyes, looked at the television and saw nothing had changed.

'Yes, you are a smart-arse!' And he laughed.

'Let's have a sanger.' He reached towards the plates, but then stopped, picked up his glass of beer and turned to me with it raised.

'Here's to you, Simian. Seems to me you're off on an adventure, having a go at the acting thing. Funny, part of me thinks I've got nowhere to go really, just feather along. But you, well, here's to you.'

And he tilted his glass of light beer in a toast.

What was it my mother said? Nobody has everything, not even Biscuit Box People. His wife had stopped her career as a teacher and had instead made a home. Nothing to be sniffed at, filling a house with love – the music, I admit, was odd – but she was a woman who could see another life like Sallyanne Atkinson who had been a mother, wife, homemaker and now was helping to change the face of this city. Such a person must have seemed transformative to many and maybe my pal's mother felt she couldn't be a part of that change, couldn't lead it, that her lanes were settled. Perhaps words spoken to yourself when you're mixing mustard in a silver serving dish were a way of being part of something bigger.

And the father, who sat in a funk watching a yacht race that didn't move, with his bung foot as evidence of an idea he had for himself, a failed ambition. What did he call himself? A fellow who had nowhere to go, just a clumsy old fossil trying to prove he could still pass muster.

They weren't big issues in the scheme of things, just stuff that happens to everybody sooner or later in a life. But I knew one thing: they weren't Biscuit Box People really. They were, as my mother had said, just people.

And as he sat there offering a toast to me with a glass of light beer, I found myself a little unsure of how I felt.

Maybe he was right. I was just a smart-arse. I wanted to say thank you and I wanted to say sorry. Instead, I said that my mum had a habit of quoting a poem, and I told the father that I think I finally understood what it was about.

'A poem?' he said.

I nodded.

As I said it out loud, I thought, yes, I did understand what it was about. It might be twee, but it made a lot more sense than the fucking King's Singers.

> We live and breathe and laugh and cry
> And learn and love and struggle and try
> And win and lose and then we die
> And at the end when it's time for goodbye
> If hearts are full of love that will tell
> Of a happy soul and a life lived well.

The father listened. 'Your mother says that?'

I said she did. 'And,' I added, 'I'm glad she does.'

He smiled, looked at the unmoving Sydney to Hobart and said very simply, 'You're a funny one, Simian, but you come from good stock.'

Then he laughed and said to me, 'Oh blow, if you can't beat the bastards, join 'em!'

He suddenly looked Race Bannon-ish.

And he began singing at the top of his lungs the chorus to 'Ob-La-Di, Ob-La-Da'. I joined in and we laughed and drank our light beer.

It wasn't long before my pal came home from work, and we headed off to our party. When we were saying goodbye, the mother stroked her husband's head and said, 'It's nice to hear you laughing again. I thought you weren't fond of the King's Singers.'

He didn't say anything but gave me a quick wink.

•

Over three and a half decades later, early in a summer, I am in Brisbane airport walking to a gate. Walking is a generous description; I have just gotten out of a moon boot after rupturing my right Achilles tendon doing a stunt on a television series. Well, that is what I tell people. I actually did it slipping over on the pavement while I was walking to get a coffee. That is about the only stunt I can do these days – getting a cup of coffee – and I can't even do that right.

My surgeon had advised me to take the moon boot with me on my trip just in case I needed it. She told me it was for security more than anything else. I didn't wear it once. Instead I carried it around as if it were a novelty tourist purchase.

I had put it down for a few minutes when I had arrived in Brisbane while I tried to find something in my bag. Much to my surprise, and I must say delight, when I went to pick it up somebody had put an empty can of Coke and a crumpled packet of chips in it. It felt good to be back in Brisbane.

As I made my way towards the gate, my name had already been called once over the PA system, I hugged the boot as I lumbered along. A bunch of people passed, and I held up the moon boot to make way for them, although it might have looked like I was using it as some form of battering ram.

As I raised it, I heard a voice say, 'Mum, it's the Redcliffe Simian!'

Me and my moon boot came to a shuddering halt, and I turned and faced a young woman with a baby hanging in a sling at her front. I remembered carrying my own children in such a sling. The baby just hung there asleep, and the young mother smiled at me. It struck me that I carried the moon boot in much the same manner as she carried her child.

Then she was joined by two people my own age, her parents.

'Kermit!' her mother said.

I stared.

'William, it's me, Rachel.'

I smiled at my old pal and then laughed.

'How are you?' we both asked of each other at the same time and we talked over each other, a little in surprise and delight, I suppose. We assured each other we were good.

She said, 'You remember my husband,' and I said I did, and me and the husband shook hands. My old pal said they had come to pick their daughter up from the airport, she was just back from Melbourne.

I said that was where I was heading and then I told the daughter I hadn't heard that old nickname in a while.

'That's what Pop said when he saw you on the TV or he had one of your books,' she said.

My old pal and her husband laughed. 'You made an impression,' she said.

Her daughter said, 'Yeah, Pop would just laugh sometimes and say, the old Redcliffe Simian, look at him go.'

'Really?' I said. 'Is he still . . . ' and I trailed off.

'No,' said my old pal. 'No, he died just after Covid.'

I said I was sorry.

My old pal said it had been hard, especially on her mum, but she was hanging in.

I wondered if her mother still played tennis.

'But, you know, he was loved, and he loved us so, yeah. It was as good as it could be.'

He had died a happy soul, just like the words of my mum's poem.

I heard my plane being called. I said I had to go. We told each other we'd have to catch up next time I was in Brisbane, or they were in Melbourne. We spoke over each other again and I wondered why old friends do that.

'That's a plan,' said my old pal.

I asked her to say hello to her mother.

She said she would, and we said goodbye.

I lumbered off and then I heard my old pal's voice. 'Kermit.'

I turned and saw she had walked up to me. She looked like she wanted to say something.

'What?' I said.

She looked at me and I thought to myself, fuck she's got the same stare as her father.

'Look, it's probably nothing, but I just wanted to tell you.' And she stopped.

I told her I really had to go.

'Dad was proud of you,' she said. 'I just thought I should tell you. Really proud.'

I stared at her. I thought of her dad. I thought of my dad. And I thought – no, I knew – I was going to cry.

She smiled, touched my shoulder and said, 'Be safe. And I'll find you.'

I walked off. I felt tears in my eyes. I went to wipe them away and I hit myself in the head with my moon boot.

I swore, then laughed and all I could think of was the frozen Sydney to Hobart and the fucking King's Singers.

Under my breath, I sang the chorus to 'Ob-La-Di, Ob-La-Da'.

4

ON THE COUCH IN REPOSE

Imagine a large late-middle-aged fellow – me – enthusiastically sprawled across a graceful lounge in much the same manner as John Singer Sargent's luscious late Impressionist portrait *Nonchaloir (Repose)*, where a beautiful woman elegantly kicks back and has a bit of a think, a ruminate if you like.

Well, I don't know what she was doing, but she does look lovely in her copiously folded white shawl; a beautiful specific moment of almost hypnotic tranquillity captured with a tactile, tangible quality.

It's a scene of everyday life and, even though that life was over a century ago, before the First World War in fact, there is a timelessness to it. It wasn't necessarily an important moment, but it is so very human. Whether I looked as lovely in my voluminous folded linen shorts and Christmas novelty t-shirt didn't really matter because I was more than happy with myself, and I was also doing something specifically unimportant.

I was engaging in a national summer ritual. I was lounging on the couch watching the Test cricket on the television, looking at a batsman walk to the crease to face the bowlers.

Travis Head was his name, and he looked to the sky in the time-honoured fashion of a player leaving the change rooms and adjusting his eyes to the light of the playing arena. I liked Travis Head. Trav. He was an old-fashioned sort of cricketer. He didn't look like a super-fit athlete; he was stocky, strong and had an out-of-time moustache. He had the air of a tradie, probably a chippie who you could trust to be on time, not rip you off but instead do a good job with a good nature.

He was a scratchy, nervous sort of a starter and would nearly always try to flick a shot off his hip through mid wicket to get off the mark. But once he got going, he could turn a game in a session and win a Test match. He had his flaws, but all in all, taken for his worth, he was a cracker, a twentieth-century Doug Walters, and he made cricket fun. Fun as.

My mother hated that expression.

'Fun as what?' she would bellow.

Fun as Trav Head.

I stared at the screen and listened without really listening to the commentators bang on about something. How much of my life has been spent like this? I thought. Lounging around watching cricket on the telly? Or listening to it on the radio.

This was not an existential moment of brooding on the passing of time and considering mortality. Remember, I was like the beauty in the folded white dress from Singer Sargent's painting – I was in repose. I knew I liked lounging and watching and listening to cricket. I just wondered how much of my existence had been spent in this pursuit.

For a game full of exact equations of figures, averages and statistics I satisfied myself with the reckoning that it was a lot, probably more time than I had actually played cricket, and I loved playing.

Playing imaginary Tests in the backyard or endless arvo games of French cricket with an old wooden tennis racquet – the whole family in the backyard, circling the batter and the tennis ball, a little yellow globe that would be belted into the heavens, through and then above the gum tree, to fly against the blue sky. Heads would crane to follow the ball's flight and then snap down to see whether it had landed safely in a pair of hands or had bounced on the ground and had to be scrambled away from barking, bounding hounds.

Playing games of cricket at school and in the street with bins as wickets where the distant poetic call of 'car coming' would signal a momentary lull in proceedings, the bin wheeled away as the driver would slowly pass with a wave of the finger or nod of the head and then the bin would be rolled back and the game would begin again.

Beach cricket, too, outfielders stationed in the water taking one-handed grasps and splashing like breaching whales. So many post-Christmas lunch games of cricket, at my wife's grandmother's, a grand old homestead in Boorowa where the circular drive doubled for the MCG; at my mother's home in Redcliffe with a phalanx of Elvis shower curtains, stocking fillers for that morning's gifts, taped to a side fence as a guitar-wielding wicketkeeper and slips cordon. At third slip, Elvis from *Flaming Star* drawing a six-shooter.

My mother saying, 'That's no way for Elvis to appeal – pointing a gun at the umpire!'

More timeless cries of 'Can I bat?', 'My turn!', 'One hand off the fence or barbie – one-hand catch' and the immortal 'Don't bowl that fast at Nanna'.

I have many memories of watching the game live too. A day spent at the recent Boxing Day Test looms large in my thoughts. It was a sellout, packed to the gunnels. I was dressed in a suit for lunch in the Long Room on a wickedly hot 40-degree day, the fans in the Members' Reserve refused to work so my suit was drenched in sweat, my mates were drenched in sweat, everybody was drenched in sweat, the whole MCG seemed to be drenched as we sat and stood and watched the debut of nineteen-year-old Sam Konstas batting against the remarkable bowler Jasprit Bumrah of India.

The boy ramped the best fast bowler in the world over his head for consecutive boundaries. There was a stunned roar then laughter and at the end of the first session, as we all turned and headed to the toilets or the bar, the confession of another suited spectator, 'I have never gone through an opening session dry, not one beer – it was that good!'

Later, as I left the MCG, I saw two others of my tribe – men who had made up for not drinking in the first session now joining a line to go to the toilet – singing a song in praise of Pat Cummins, the Australian captain. They were singing it to the theme of an old kids' TV show, *Postman Pat*.

Captain Pat, Captain Pat,
Captain Pat in his baggy green cap.

They sang those two phrases over and over, and before too long, the whole toilet queue of men was singing it in a celebratory bellow. The chant began echoing around the walkways.

On my way out I walked along with a laughing mate, The Dog. 'I used to sing that Postman Pat song to the boys when they were young,' he said.

He was talking of his two sons, now fully grown. Apart from being a grand pal and dogged cricketer, The Dog was himself a postie.

He smiled a little. 'Long time ago . . . It's a catchy tune. Those lads at the pisser should try to come up with another verse.'

We both laughed and then suddenly before us was a very old man who was obviously not well. His skin was very pale and he was in a wheelchair, wearing a mask attached to an oxygen bottle. A younger man, not far off our age, was pushing him.

They reached a lift, other punters gently making way for them, and I held the lift door open for them. The younger man nodded his thanks while the older man in the wheelchair took off his mask and said to me, 'A gentleman and a scholar you are, sir!'

One of my pals said, 'I don't know about that, but he has his moments.'

The old man laughed a little.

Just before the door closed, the old man took the hand of the younger man and said softly, 'What a wonderful day. I do love you, boy.'

The younger man held the old man's hand softly. 'Love you too, Dad.'

The door closed and the lift descended.

My mate The Dog said, almost to himself, 'Fuck I love the cricket.'

•

Yes, I think to myself, I love the cricket too. And, lounging on the couch, it feels so lovely watching THE cricket. Cricket needs that definite article: THE. It is something specific; a specific moment – just like the painting of *Repose.*

The first time I can remember watching the cricket was as a six-year-old. One afternoon we sat and watched black-and-white images from Perth where a young batsman, tall and dark-haired, made his debut. He stood at the crease, leaning with an elegant angle to his stance, and managed to score a century. It was Greg Chappell, and he was quickly surrounded by hundreds of grown-ups and kids who ran onto the field to slap him on the back or to shake his hand.

My sisters were happy, I remember. They shouted, 'Gregory did it!'

My mother said that made him sound like a Pope. 'All those Gregorys.'

'Or a Peck,' said one of my sisters. As in the movie actor Gregory Peck.

'Oh, I don't think he's a Gregory, he is more a Greg,' from my mother.

'Whatever you call him, he is a keeper,' my father muttered. 'He'll be around for a while, just like his brother.'

His brother was Ian Chappell and the next time I watched the cricket was when Ian Chappell had been made the Captain of Australia for the unprecedented seventh Test, organised to make up for a washed-out sixth Test.

There was an unprecedented argument in our house over whether to watch the cricket, which I couldn't quite understand because my sisters had been more than happy to watch the cricket and Gregory/Greg Chappell before.

Not this time. They wanted to watch another channel that was showing, on alternating days, old re-runs of two medical dramas about two doctors, one called Dr Kildare played by a man called Richard Chamberlain who was very tall and good-looking but also incredibly wooden. The other doctor did away with the professional prefix and was called Ben Casey played by Vince Edwards, a brooding, stocky dark-haired fellow with incredibly hairy forearms and an incredibly bad temper.

My mother said Richard Chamberlain's Dr Kildare was the sort of person who might work in a Mathers shoe shop while my Aunty Rita asserted Ben Casey was just like the bloke who had the butcher's shop at Deception Bay. 'Lovely butcher, but you've got to watch out for those hairy arms – very easy for a stray hair to end up in the mince!'

On the day in question the age-old conundrum of 'Why do we have to watch the cricket all the time?' raised its hoary old head.

My sisters' logic was quite obvious: both the doctors' show only went for one hour; surely it would be okay to watch Richard from Mathers shoe shop or Vince from the Deception Bay butchers and then switch back to the cricket.

One of them stood up and walked to the television and turned the channel by gripping the knob of the channel selector and turning it a number of notches. This was in the days before remotes and when the channel was turned there was a soft clunking sound as the selector did its business.

It wasn't unknown for some member of the family to be the designated channel turner on any given day, though somehow my mother was usually the trusted helmsman of the channels, navigating the living room through stormy seas.

These sorts of duties were handed out to keep the house running. One of the other tasks that was shared around was somebody being urged to 'Call the dogs' when the hounds of the battleaxe block became slightly annoying when up and about.

But the TV stand-off was a ritual in itself. As soon as one of my sisters had turned the channel to the doctor show my brother stood up and walked slowly to the television and turned the channel selector back to the ABC, or Channel 2, the broadcaster of the cricket.

Back and forth they went, sitting up, turning the channel selector, then sitting down. Soon there was a split in the ranks. My youngest sister said she wouldn't mind watching the Pope – meaning Greg Chappell – bat again if that was a possibility.

'No!' said my eldest sister. 'They're going to lose anyway; it said so on the radio.'

My brother stood up and joined my sister, each of them standing either side of the telly. It was going to a switch-off!

Then my father said. 'Come on now, it is the Ashes.'

My sister protested with, 'But the radio said they weren't going to win.'

My father thought for a moment and then tried a tactic that had been successful in the past. 'Can you watch your doctor until an ad comes on and then we can see what's happening in the cricket?'

My sister held the channel selector. 'Oh, that one. Last time you said that when the first Leo Muller ad came on we went to THE cricket and stayed there.'

'It was a Leach Motors ad,' another sister corrected.

My sister with her fingers on the channel selector laughed. 'I don't care, it was a car ad, and I know Da's tricks!'

My father half laughed and then harrumphed; his ploy being unmasked.

It was all rather fun.

It was left to my mother to dispense Solomon-like wisdom.

'Give the bleeding knob-turner a turn!' Knob-turner being her term for the channel selector. 'Now, which doctor do you like more, Richard from Mathers or old hairy arms from Deception Bay?'

'Richard from Mathers.'

'Right, if he's on we'll watch that, if not it's THE cricket.'

This sounded fair to everyone and there was murmured agreement as if the national cabinet had decided on a course of management over a tricky decision.

'Oh, it's Leo Muller!' said somebody as the car dealership advertisement came to its singsong end.

Richard from Mathers, Hairy Arms from Deception Bay butchers or the cricket? High stakes indeed.

We all stared at the telly. Then onto the screen came a funny high voice and written symbols on a blackboard.

'Man,' said the voice. The symbol of man.

'Woman.' The symbol of a woman.

'Earth.' And a drawing that looked a little like a would-be UNICEF Christmas card. The symbol of the Earth.

'We'll have to take his word for that,' mumbled my father.

'Death.' And a drawn cross symbolising a cross and death.

Then finally the high voice said, 'Infinity.' And then a drawn number 8 lying on its side.

'Infinity,' my sisters groaned. 'That means THE cricket.'

My father almost yelled, 'Yes, it's old Hairy Arms!'

Ben Casey was on, and before we even knew what the medical drama was that old Hairy Arms from Deception Bay butchery had to confront, the knob-turner landed on a shimmering image of a cricket ground and then, for the first time I can remember, I heard a high voice not too dissimilar to the beginning of Ben Casey.

'Welcome back to the Sydney Cricket Ground for the afternoon session of the seventh Ashes Test.'

It was Richie Benaud. That funny singsong but also tuneless, high, clipped Australian voice was Richie Benaud.

From somewhere around the house, my sister cried, 'Infinity!'

And it was true, watching the cricket seemed to stretch on forever. But sometimes forever can be eventful and that Test had it all: drunken members of the crowd hanging over the fence grabbing the English fast bowler John Snow on the boundary line after the Australian leg spinner Terry Jenner had ducked into a Snow short ball; the ground being littered with cans and bottles; the English captain Ray Illingworth looking like an angry manual arts teacher and leading his team off the ground. And that voice of Richie Benaud's, which somehow would be forever connected to the beginning of old Hairy Arms the Deception Bay butcher's medical drama, gave Illingworth a bit of character assessment.

'And Illingworth in this case, arguing with the referee, is behaving more in the manner of a prima donna from a South American football club than the captain of a touring team.'

Watching the cricket.

All those summers, all those voices.

On the ABC radio cricket commentary, people like Drew Morphett and Jim Maxwell would chuckle like slightly dodgy and daggy older uncles about where they ate last night and how they went with the double at some faraway race meetings.

The commentary seemed more suited to some slightly tipsy club lunch than a sporting contest, but it was important enough to blanket the national broadcaster's main network airwaves.

But it was the cricket voices on the TV that were the most fun because they were so normal and untrained but at the same time quite eccentric – especially the matter-of-factness of Ian Chappell. I'd love to hear him announce the end of life as we know it. It would sound like a bloke giving you street instructions.

'And. Uh. Now. After the end . . . of the . . . uh . . . over. All life and uh civilisation . . . as we . . . uh. Know it. Will end . . . Well, there you . . . uh, go.'

The beautiful Caribbean cadence of Tony Cozier, liltingly in step with the sparse poetry of Richie Benaud.

Ah, Richie Benaud. He was my mother's favourite cricketer. 'Him running in to bowl with his collar up and his shirt unbuttoned down to his ankles. Smashing.'

His voice became a background to summer. Though over the years the otherworldly tones of Richie Benaud began to sound more and more like an Antipodean cousin of Yoda.

Eventually the commentators can't control themselves and they become almost fans. Richie's strangled, 'He's done it – Yes!' describing the effect of a well-concealed flipper from a leg spinner sounded more like an unsuccessful attempt to stifle a barely controlled orgasm.

The same for Bill Lawry who would excitedly scream, 'Yes – got him! Neck and crop,' like some half-mad scientist discovering a new chemical element and enjoying himself way too much.

Another voice from Richie's playing days was Frank 'Typhoon' Tyson, who sounds like a made-up name for a boxer from a very bad Elvis Presley movie.

Typhoon was apparently the fastest bowler Benaud had ever seen in his playing days and the Englishman skittled the Australians in the 1954–55 series in the Australian summer.

He didn't play that long and ended up immigrating to Australia where he began a long and successful career as a teacher of classics and English at Carey Grammar School – and also as a commentator. He had a rich, deep voice from the English north that had been softened by years of well-heeled education.

He often read the works of Chaucer, Virginia Woolf and Arnold Bennett on tour. Keith Miller, the dashing Australian all-rounder, politely called him a Pommy bastard.

Typhoon sledged back, not in profanity but in Wordsworth poetry.

For still, the more he works, the more

Do his weak ankles swell!

Keith happily responded, 'All right, so you're a smart bastard, but you're still a Pommy bastard.'

Frank used to add a bit of richness and depth to the cricket. He often sounded like some wise old admiral plotting the sinking of the *Bismarck* or, if cricket was ever a TV medical drama, an ancient professor advising Richie Benaud's chief surgeon character. Although, in the Redcliffe Universe, Richie would undoubtedly not work in Mathers with Richard or at the butcher's with hairy arms Vince, no — most likely he'd be the owner of Pierre's Mill, the restaurant with the windmill in front of the Redcliffe drive-in. That's about as French as the peninsula got.

And in truth, Pierre was a Dutch bloke — hence the windmill on the roof — but everybody just assumed he was French for some reason.

Typhoon's greatest effort was appearing on camera, besuited, bald as a baboon's arse and in deep, rich and fruity tones stating, 'There is the drama . . . the pitch!' It was entertainingly ridiculous, and my brother and I still say that phrase to each other over the phone in random conversation.

For me, the flogging of tacky 'poolroom' cricket memorabilia — 'Tastefully framed and finished!'— has always been a guilty delight, although it does sound odd and a little sad without the late Tony Greig.

Greig always seemed to be playing things up quite a bit and I suppose those cartoonish qualities are picked up by a mass-broadcasting medium and can hide the real person. The quite amazing thing about Tony Greig was that such a crossbred voice – English, South African and Australian vowels all mixed together – should embed itself as a sound of our summer.

•

Many years ago, when Mark 'Tubby' Taylor was Australian cricket captain, my wife asked me what I was doing and I said, 'Watching the cricket.' She came into the room and summed up the situation according to her.

Taylor was standing at first slip, while Glenn McGrath was stalking back to his mark to bowl. Tubby stood with his arms folded across his ample frame, chewing gum. Occasionally picking his nose or scratching himself in the nether regions. I sprawled on the couch and picked and scratched in company.

My wife said, 'You're watching a well-fed man chew with his mouth open, pick his nose, spit and scratch himself in public in an almost criminal manner. Is that what you're doing?'

I nodded and said slowly, 'I'm watching the cricket.'

'What?' my wife asked with a hint of incredulity.

I pointed to the figure of Mark Taylor on the screen. 'Watching the cricket.'

Tubby continued to pick and scratch.

My wife shook her head and left me to it.

In a way we were both right. If you saw someone standing at a bus stop behaving the way Tubby, or any number of cricketers, behave during the game you'd probably call for the suitable authorities. But those who knew the game, like me, knew better. Tubby was playing cricket.

Ridiculous really, but there you have it.

What Tubby was doing was a part of the wonder of enjoying cricket. And when you're watching or listening to the game, you have to appreciate that as much as catching, hitting, throwing and running.

Well, not really, but it would be interesting to see a highlights package from over the years of former champions taking wickets, scoring runs and taking catches but also picking noses, spitting and tugging at crotches.

It is understandable why they do this – it is a physical activity and when you exert yourself stuff happens – but I can't recall seeing as much excavation and expectoration as we see today.

I lie on my couch and think it is most likely because the television cameras are everywhere these days: multi angles, slow motion and something called Hawk-Eye where a suspended camera floats over the players. There are cameras everywhere. Broadcasters can't help themselves, even feeling the compunction to show footage of competitors in the change rooms.

Watching a 'fly on the wall' documentary about the men's Test team became irritating because I found the shots of Australian Test cricketers in the dressing sheds more a construct than bearing any insight or reality. It was an intrusion that didn't add anything to the doco because the players would have known there were cameras present, so how unguarded and real could it be?

I didn't see one fondle, spit or nose-pick in that doco.

As I look at Travis Head walking out to bat with an unaccountably nervous and scratchy Steve Smith – fidgeting, gesticulating where he should have hit the ball, talking to himself – Trav seems solid and dependable.

Ian Chappell used to come out to bat like that, with his collar popped and a baggy green on his head. How I loved and still adore a popped collar.

I remember my father defending the wonderful Ian Chappell at the crease. Chappelli, as he was known, had the habit of constantly adjusting his protector as he batted and my mother would say, 'That lad should either wash himself properly or be locked up.'

'Come on now, love, the man is thinking. Planning.'

My mother snorted.

'Richie would never do that sort of thing on the field. He may have worn shirts in the same way but he never behaved that way.'

My father always thought Richie Benaud a bit too French, a little too sophisticated with unbuttoned shirts to the ankles and not a hair out of place. Richie liked the ballet and the opera and fine wine and, in my father's words, 'Had a great cricket mind but a lower lip like a Frog, made for cheese and wine and the finer things.'

Like me, my father was an Ian Chappell man.

'We can't all be like Rodin's "Thinker", sitting there with his head in his hands,' he said. 'Cricket is dynamic. Ian Chappell's thinking about the game, meditating. Planning.'

My mother laughed.

'Colin, the boy is fiddling with himself . . . and certain people tend to copy certain things.'

She tilted her head towards me. My father was going to say something else but right then Ian Chappell must have had some very deep thought pass through his mind because he attacked his protector with his gloved hand like a man trying to put out a fire.

My father, knowing that Ian Chappell was my favourite cricketer, turned and looked at me. Then he looked at my mother and turned back to me with some blunt advice: 'Don't you be doing that in public. Chappelli can get away with it, but you? You'll get arrested.'

Annette Kellerman-ed again!

Now, all these years later, when you watch fidgety Steve Smith or Marnus Labuschagne at the crease, Chappelli and Mark Taylor seem the height of propriety.

Not everyone likes cricket and even some who've played the game at the highest level, like Steve Smith and Ian Chappell, have said they don't enjoy watching the game. For them the joy is in playing the game.

I understand. I loved playing the game too, but for me and many others summer wouldn't be complete without 'watching the cricket'.

The element that some people miss about watching the cricket is that of repose. Of being lost a little in your thoughts as you lounge and watch.

Sometimes it's provoked by what you see on the telly. There's a break at the end of the over and there's a short ad flogging an upcoming doco about Australian cricket. The former fast bowler Mitchell Johnson appears with his Viva Zapata moustache. And I say to myself, 'Where you are is where you are.' It's an old saying and I've always taken it to mean whatever you may think you might be, whatever you may have achieved in life – rewards, success, whatever – where you are at a given moment is where you are.

So, you accept it and get on with life.

Nothing like getting about with the punters to bear that old saying out. I was at a pleasant bookshop signing a large quantity of 'stock' with a slightly younger version of myself on the cover. I chatted to a staff member who told me how Mitchell Johnson had been in the shop earlier signing his book.

'I liked Mitchell Johnson,' I said.

The staff member nodded. 'Yeah, top bloke, really down to earth.'

'That's nice to know,' I said.

'We could do with him now in the Tests.'

'Depends on which Mitch turned up,' I said. Consistency was always a bit of a question with Mitch but when he was on song, he was unstoppable. I looked up from signing and saw a woman looking at me.

The way she looked at me made me stop signing.

The look was slightly hard to explain. Her face was scrunched into a half scowl.

It was a look someone might give if you'd just farted or erupted in some other bodily function.

We looked at each other.

I knew I hadn't farted or belched or hiccupped, but I felt a twinge about the big Indian feast I'd had the night before.

Could I trust the vindaloo?

I smiled a little but she still stared.

'Who . . .' she said slowly, 'are you?'

Good then, no need to fear a high-volume body-eruption embarrassment.

She was trying to work out who I was.

I introduced myself and held up the copy of my latest book. She looked at it then back to me.

'Oh.' She nodded. 'You. I remembered you when you were slimmer.'

Well, where you are being where you are, I couldn't pretend that at this particular moment there wasn't an overwhelming body of evidence of me having spent a lot of time in a very good paddock.

Later that day, walking through a city lane, I passed a man standing in front of a reflective wall. He was unkempt and obviously living rough. He was staring at his reflection and saying over and over to himself, 'It's your fault, your fault, your fault you're here.'

I walked past. Stopped, looked back. I asked him if he was all right.

He just stared at the wall, mumbling.

I asked again.

He stared.

I walked on.

Where you are being where you are.

Sometimes that can be a place you might never have thought you'd end up.

Wearing the baggy green of the national men's cricket team in a Test match, a dream of players and a daydream or fanciful wish for many of this nation's population, and then you find yourself being the butt of national jokes like Mitchell

Johnson. Having to put up with the endless moronic chants of the Barmy Army.

Or being stared at by someone who remembered when you were slimmer and younger. You can laugh, or maybe you can't.

It can be a bit confronting. There are ways back from where you are. Look at Mitch Johnson, written off a couple of times only to come back to end his cricket career on his terms, to live his life as he wanted to, as much as anybody can.

There on the couch, as I watch the cricket, I think about the man in the city lane blaming his reflection. Where you are is where you are. It can be tough.

Where I am is where I am and that is lounging on the couch watching the cricket.

Travis has tucked a shot off his hip as predicted and the ball floats tantalisingly close to an elegant-looking Indian fielder but falls short. Trav is being Trav.

Steve Smith is more eccentric than ever – he is nearing ten thousand runs in Test cricket and I can tell he is nervous. Funny how such an experienced player can still get nervous, but we all get nervous I suppose. A ball rears and he plays some inexplicably stupid shot and he's out, caught in the gully. If that had been the cordon of Elvises in my mother's back-yard that long-ago Christmas, it would have been a cheekily smiling Elvis with his captain's hat on from *Girls! Girls! Girls!*

The commentators blame the pitch. The pitch. The last defence before accepting any personal responsibility.

The welcome nasally tones of Mark Waugh beg to differ. 'I think the wicket is playing better now than it did in the first dig, just a poor shot.'

Mark Waugh would be a good commentator to sit with that classic collection of suburban voices of my younger days.

Blame the pitch.

That's what the well-rounded vowel commentators from the ABC like Norman May said about the wicket in the first Ashes Test of the 1974–75 series, when Australian pace duo Jeff Thomson and Dennis Lillee rattled the English batsmen to their back teeth and very marrow.

There were several highlights.

Some of Norman May's calling was entertainingly off: 'Oh, what a lovely shot, and . . . he's . . . out!'

Or when an English batsman got his hair parted with a cricket ball flying at nearly 100 miles per hour all Norman could muster was, 'Well, that was a nasty one.'

Captain Ian Chappell made a belligerent ninety on the first day and argued with the lanky South Africa–born English all-rounder Tony Greig, who seemed to like to argue with every Australian, including Lillee, who he unwisely bounced.

The Australian fast bowlers' response, when it was England's turn to bat, was so frighteningly quick and entertaining, it seemed slightly unfair to glory so much in the looks on English faces.

Television coverage wasn't great back then – just a camera at either end – but you could almost smell the fear those poor players exuded. Even gutsy ones such as Greig and John Edrich.

But the thing I remembered most was the way my father was sure England wouldn't win this particular match. 'Clem's sorted it for sure,' I heard him saying one afternoon just before the Test. He was talking about Clem Jones, the former Brisbane Lord Mayor and curator of the Gabba wicket.

Clem Jones, everyone loved him.

When I called my mother to tell her of my son's birth she said, 'What did you call it?'

'Clement, Clem for short,' I said.

'Oh, lovely,' cooed my mother down the line. 'After Clem Jones or one of the Popes?'

Before I could say anything else she bellowed back her approval. 'Doesn't matter, a lovely name and he'll live a useful life like our Clem!' Meaning Clem Jones.

Clem Jones was, like my Old Man, a Labor man. And in the dark days of long-serving premier Joh Bjelke-Petersen, however bad things might have seemed, there was always Clem. He was the first man to produce a comprehensive town plan and a vision for Brisbane and was one of the architects of the wonderful city it has become. He helped sewer and pave the streets of the state capital and was instrumental in winning the right to host the 1982 Commonwealth Games after an unsuccessful pitch for the 1978 Games.

He was also a fellow who could turn his hand to almost anything, including cricket-pitch curating. Clem was a huge cricket fan and quite an influential administrator, being just as likely to turn up at the Gabba working the turnstiles as making major decisions such as the removal of the Gabba's then-curator before that first Ashes Test. The wicket was instead curated by Clem, who produced a pitch he memorably described as 'a bit crook at one end'.

Whichever end it was, nobody was sure, for one seemed as bad as the other. It didn't really matter with the way Lillee and Thomson bowled, and that first Test sparked a wonderful summer and a high point in Australian cricket.

Clem's involvement with the first Test was a unique example of sport and politics mixing, but it's also a reminder of another time, another Brisbane, another Queensland, when nobody was too big or important, no matter what office they might have held, to get down in the trenches and get their hands dirty.

Colourful characters abounded, but not all of the politics and civics of the 1970s and 1980s were about backhanders and corruption, and even though my dad wasn't that well when he finally saw Wayne Goss win in 1989 for the ALP, he always contented himself there were good people on the opposite side of his political fence. People such as Terry White, Gordon Chalk, Llew Edwards and Mike Ahern. Names some may not remember, but they were good 'uns.

And there was always Clem. After he left politics, he never tired of civic life, becoming chairman of the Darwin Reconstruction Commission convened to rebuild Darwin after the devastation of Cyclone Tracy in 1974. He worked constantly on behalf of various charities and on his death in December 2007 he left enormous amounts to their ongoing support.

It's too easy to lump politicians together, to brand them all the same and say they don't count. The good ones who live good lives do, even if a wicket they produce for a Test match is a bit crook at one end.

Why blame the wicket? What's the point? And then Mark Waugh, nicknamed Junior because he was the younger twin to his elder brother, former Australian captain Steve Waugh, nasally agrees with me.

'Well, they've just got to play on what they've been given to play on.'

Thanks, Junior. Where you are is where you are.

Travis Head is joined by a new batsman with a name like a Gary Cooper cowboy character, Beau Webster, an enormous man who also has an old-fashioned out-of-time head. If Trav and his mo screamed the seventies and the eighties then

Big Beau would easily be at home in one of Don Bradman's teams, so steadfast and block-faced does he seem with his short back and sides and big chin. The only jarring element being a shiny ear stud the size of Tasmania in his great earlobe.

Webster is, incidentally, from Tasmania, from a town called Snug, and his nickname is Slug. The Slug from Snug.

Slug from Snug and Trav have things in hand it seems and they belt balls rather effectively on what is supposed to be a bad wicket.

I watch, satisfied, but know that this is the last Test of the summer and that 'watching the cricket' will end soon. All things end, I think, and I'll just have to find something else to while away the hours.

And then I hear rain on the roof above. And even though the Test is in a sunny Sydney there is rain on the roof above me here in my home. Such a lovely sound. And I am so comfortable on the couch, I doze.

And whether it's a memory or a dream I can't quite decide but I recall another summer night and rain. A storm.

Early on in our relationship, my future wife Sarah Watt wasn't sure what she wanted from me. 'Maybe it's just nice to have a summer fling? What do you think?' She looked at me with her lovely watchful eyes.

I had no real idea what was going on, but I was enjoying myself so much I just nodded.

She frowned slightly.

Later that night there was a storm, a summer special there on the beach at Austinmer, south of Sydney.

We both liked stormy weather, but we began to have a fight. Not a bad one, just an argument about something that seemed to be a mask for something else.

I couldn't keep up with what we were fighting about and just threw up my hands and walked out. I walked down to the beach. I walked through the rain, the waves pounding on the shore and then I went out to the end of the rectangular sea pool that sat at one end of Austinmer beach.

Two lights at either corner gave off a hazy golden glow in the howling rain. Waves crashed over the pool wall, drenching me. I stood there and realised something. I turned and started running along the concrete and then stopped, for running through the lights was Sarah Watt.

I looked at her and I laughed.

She stopped running just after passing through the hazy golden light and she shouted, 'Are you laughing at the way I run?'

'No.' I paused. 'No, I'm happy. And I don't want to be a summer fling.'

'Neither do I,' she said, and she walked closer.

And there in the rain, we kissed. I told her for the first, but certainly not the last time, that I loved her.

Rain on the roof above and I come out of my reverie. I am so blissfully happy at that memory that I almost cry. I think I will.

And then, I hear the cricket.

'Shot!' cries Junior.

I look up and see that Slug from Snug and Trav are doing Australia proud. And I am happy. All things pass, even when in repose on the couch. But somehow watching the cricket makes it – life, I suppose – seem simply at that specific unimportant moment so very right and lovely.

5

OPEN SEASON

Midsummer in Australia is a fallow period where not much happens; everyone seems to be somewhere else, like down the beach or in the sticks, not even really on holidays, just away.

Even people who stay at home are somewhere else in early January.

It's a mindset more than anything else. People want to be away from their usual lives. Everyone switches off for those few weeks and, even though people may be happily occupying themselves, there is something brewing in the background of this fallow summer stage, a common thread that fills a quiet moment, a conversation starter, a headline from the exclamation people.

What's the something? Or rather the somethings. Enter the three sporting events of Australian summer that are the backdrop to life. People may not engage in them, may even detest them, but we all know they are happening – there's simply no getting away from them.

As soon as they come, there is a clamour for involvement. And after they have finished, there is nothing left, just as if a carnival has come and gone.

We've already spoken about the Boxing Day Test and the Sydney to Hobart Yacht Race. The other event is, of course, the Australian Open Tennis.

Around this time, it's not unusual to have conversations like the one I had with someone who would be best termed a 'work colleague'. I was still in the away-with-the-pixies-during-the-January-somewhere-else phase, and I admit I had been woken from a rather pleasant arvo snooze so wasn't as sharp as I could have been.

My phone rings. I pick it up and take the call.

'Hey, how are you?' says the work colleague.

'Hello there, not too foul. How are you – good?' I reply.

'Pretty good. You going to the AO?'

I think for a moment. The extent of my relationship with this work colleague has been as voices on either ends of a digital connection. I don't really know him, and I assume that he must like music. Theatre. If he's talking about the opera. The Australian Opera.

'Well, I don't go much. But when I do it's usually worth it. Great music and gorgeous costumes.'

There is a pause. Have I said something to offend him? 'Okay, yeah . . . I guess so.' He has a slightly bewildered tone now.

I push on. 'What's playing? Something on in the park?'

There is another pause that goes on and becomes awkward.

'Ah, they are playing . . . at the tennis thing, the tennis park . . . aren't they?' says the work colleague.

Now I pause. 'Are . . . you . . . talking about the opera? The AO?'

'No,' comes the rather curt reply. 'The tennis. The Australian Open.'

'Right,' I say. 'Of course . . . ' I am left hanging and then say, a little pathetically, 'Do you ever go to the opera?'

'No, never.' The work colleague is very curt now.

'Well, how have you been enjoying the tennis?'

'I haven't. I don't really watch it. But it's everywhere. Just assumed you should ask people about it . . . it's a Melbourne thing, isn't it? I mean it's a thing everywhere. Isn't it? Just a bit of banter,' says the work colleague.

I slowly say, 'Right, yes, yeah.'

There is a pause and then it's all business. 'Look, the costume department want to know if your measurements have changed. You put on any weight?'

'No, don't think so.'

'Great . . . well, enjoy the tennis.'

'Thanks,' I say, and add, 'Enjoy the opera.'

He laughs.

The tennis is one of those carnivals that hits town and draws people's attention. 'It's everywhere, isn't it?' the work colleague had said. And he was right. The Australian Open is everywhere for those days it's on: broadcasters, organisers, the sponsors and the exclamation mark people want it to be everywhere, but nobody could have imagined the reach would be so extensive that the tennis would even invade the world of a make-believe crime centre.

One summer night in January 1994, a new television drama was to debut. The broadcaster of the new drama, Channel Seven, was also the broadcaster of the tennis and they decided the Australian Open would piggyback the show.

It was put to me once, circa 1994 in fact, by a director friend, that if Australian television networks were retail chains then Channel Nine would be Myer, Channel Ten would be Best and Less and Channel Seven would be Kmart. Channel Nine always looked pretty flashy, Channel Ten certainly didn't pay for any fancy overheads and Channel Seven was full of shitty knock-offs of Channel Nine products that usually broke when you tried to use them. Oh, and they also had a lot of sport.

The two public broadcasters were given short shrift: SBS would be an exotic deli and the ABC would be a not-for-profit charity.

Whether or not there was any accuracy to this is open to some conjecture but on the night of the eighteenth of January there may have been a skerrick of truth in things being slightly bung at Channel Seven.

The TV drama was set in a country town in Victoria, a place with a generic-sounding name, and was about the local police who served there. They were kept ridiculously busy with all manner of crime, from mysteries about cake-baking competitions, missing people, missing animals, mine shaft collapses, ghostly bushrangers, sieges, rigged shearing competitions, broken hearts and betrayals, beauty pageant kidnapping, sieges, murders, theft, mysterious crop circles and UFOs, more sieges, even ninjas in the local hospital. Oddly though, there were never any episodes with crimes involving tennis.

Until the night when the police drama in the country town premiered. The suits at the Melbourne station invited the 'creatives' — the cast, a few directors and the producers — to the fabled seventh-floor boardroom, which could have doubled as a baronial banquet hall from some Wagnerian opera.

Nibbles and drinks were provided, and the assembled collection prepared to watch the show rolling out live on air as Australia was introduced to the characters and crimes of this country town. And the tennis.

About halfway through the episode, when the kindly sergeant was solving crime by reading a newspaper, he looked up to see the new young police constable entering the station. As he folded the paper to greet her there was a popping sound that at first matched the folding but then didn't. Then he seemed to emit an ear-splitting grunt, followed by more of the hard popping sound and then another grunt and an even harder popping sound — this went on as he walked with his folded paper under his arm with his lips moving but no words coming from them.

Then there was a cry of 'Out!', a communal groan and then applause. Everyone looked at the big screen on the wall.

'A nice tie-in with the tennis,' some suit said. Then one of the producers said meekly, 'Is that going out live?'

'Certainly is,' said another suit with hair almost as tall as the broadcasting tower. 'It's going out live.' He elongated 'live' to stress its importance.

The producer looked at him.

'Liiiiiiiiiiiiiiiiive,' said High Hair suit, reassuring the producer.

'With the tennis audio?' said the producer, sounding quite sickly.

There was a stillness that stretched on until another popping sound, another grunt and a cow stood in a paddock.

'Jesus Christ on a bicycle!' shouted a suit and every one of them, save one who was too slow, grabbed a phone handset – this was in the days before mobile phones were commonplace. So old handsets were grabbed like weapons aboard a pirate ship about to go into battle – and into the handpiece yabbering mouths shrieked rapidly, words tumbling over each other, the sounds of grunting and tennis balls being smacked to and fro across the court, the applause of the spectators, the chair umpires scoring and the odd line or two from the commentators, sometimes whispered, sometimes declamatory, 'This is what people come to see!' – and all the while the suits talked over each other, High Hair repeating over again, 'Christ! Oh, Christ Oh Jesus Christ!'

And all the while on screen in the fictional country town, crimes were serenaded with the room's cacophony of noise.

The phoneless suit had an inspired moment and grabbed the air phone that was used to talk to the security desk or the kitchen and he shrieked into the mouthpiece. Lord knows what the kitchen or the security guard made of the noise but at least air phone suit had armed himself with a weapon.

On screen there's argy bargy in the pub, then a dog barking and then dishevelled police officers and there's an old coot behind a screen door and there is another grunt, a racquet hit and the little suit with the big High Hair saying into his phone, 'Christ Jesus Christ. The tennis is on, the tennis sounds are on over the top of the soapie – we can see the soapie, but we are hearing the tennis.'

One of the producers, a large man dressed in a fishing vest, said, 'It's a procedural drama, not a soapie.'

High Hair looked at him. 'I don't care what the fuck the thing is, it's got the tennis noise! Jesus Christ!'

The general manager of the station put down his phone handset with a flourish, stood and raised his hand. 'It's all right, it's all right! Shush now, it's all right.'

One by one the suits stopped shrieking, save for the air phone suit, who had seemingly made contact with the kitchen and so decided to order a snack on the sly while all the hullaballoo had gone on.

Sadly for him, he hadn't noticed the sudden silence and so he was heard to say, rather conspiratorially, 'A ham and cheese toastie with extra cheese please . . .' And, unmasked, he trailed off as High Hair, who was more senior to air phone suit, said for the twentieth time, 'Jesus Christ!' and shot air phone a withering look.

'Shush!' said the general manager of the station, 'it's all right.'

There was a pause, the sound of a tennis ball being bounced, and the general manager said proudly, 'It's all right – it's a Sydney fuck-up, they've got the wrong lines punched – we're fine. We're in the clear!'

There was a grunt, a serve, another grunt, the serve was a winner, there was a gasp from the crowd and the umpire awarding points.

The general manager said heartily, 'Good shot! Let's have more drinks.'

And just as quickly as the suits picked up the phones, they put them down and helped themselves to another drink.

The network had to replay the show two nights later with the proper audio. But who knows, the tennis may have helped because the show, *Blue Heelers*, became a huge success, running for nearly twelve years. Game, set and match.

•

Today, the tennis is still everywhere. There's always a handful of 'Aussie hopes' who are heralded as they make their way through the opening rounds but soon thin out to one plucky Aussie battler who squeaks into the fourth round, if they are lucky.

Everybody is supposed to be behind them, according to the exclamation mark people, until the plucky battler, usually some intense young person, is summarily dismissed from proceedings by a top-tier player.

Does anybody really get behind them these days though? Tennis players are otherworldly, like a cross between soccer players and ballet dancers, nearly always neatly attired, paid a fortune and with quite a robotic manner.

Sure, some may break a few racquets or grunt like a bull in rut, or shriek as if they have just been pushed from a great height, but it has become very formulaic. It's an odd sport. You can't cheer continuously; you have to remain hushed and mindful of the competitor's preparation to serve, the seconds stretching on as the players gather themselves. Silence must be maintained while they ply their trade.

It's a bit precious, like golf, where commentators have to whisper in hushed and awed tones as if they are in a cathedral. And if the players are the clergy – watch out! – because those holier-than-thou clergy of the court can pump the air, scream at themselves, scream at their coaches, scream to the universe, as if – as Mum used to say about the odd people who carried on at the bus stop across from our home after missing a bus – they are not quite right, whether they have just missed the ten past ten across the bridge to Sandgate station or a backhand drive down the line.

And yet all they do is hit a yellow ball away from and to each other.

Almost everybody seems like they came out of the same tennis test tube. Even the peculiar Novak Djokovic, an incredibly intense athlete, with those close-together eyes and limbs seemingly made of rubber bending this way and flexing that way. He could only ever be a tennis player.

Down the beach, as one invariably is during summer, when you are drying yourself off, people gather in chatty little clumps. There is an old bloke with a beautiful pop-eyed old blue heeler cattle dog, and somebody asks the question that is ubiquitous at this time of year. 'Been watching the tennis?'

The old bloke with the old blue heeler shook his head. 'I tried to give it a go, but I don't know. Hard to get round anybody. Miss people like Ash Barty, she was a ripper.'

'There's lots of good players, still,' said a red-haired woman. I remembered her from the last summer when I had stomped down to the beach after watching Australia collapse against the West Indies in the last Test of the summer at the Gabba. I hadn't been able to bear to look at it any longer and was still shaking my head as I walked into the water. A woman already in the drink looked at me and said, 'Come on, the beach is supposed to make everything better.'

I nodded but said, 'It will — just have to get over a batting collapse.'

She laughed. 'Don't start me! I just got in to calm down.'

That made me laugh and I did feel much better.

The old bloke with the old bluey nodded and said yes, he knew there were lots of good players in the tournament, but he just couldn't come at them. 'I like players like Ash Barty, real people.'

'What do you mean, real people?' laughed the red-headed woman, who incidentally had a nice laugh.

'Well, I can imagine 'em being something else as well as a tennis player. Ash Barty always made me feel like she would be a good nurse. The same as Pat Rafter, I always thought he was like a nurse – good, caring people.'

Another fellow my age who lived around the corner asked about Lleyton Hewitt. 'What would he be?'

'Oh, Lleyton would be a landscape gardener, I'd say.'

The idea that Lleyton Hewitt would be yelling, 'Come on!' after successfully laying garden pavers or removing stubborn clumps of blackberry made me smile.

'You just deal with Aussie players?' I asked.

'Oh, they are just some I like. Like to back home-grown. I liked all those Swedes back in the day, always had a soft spot for some of the Yanks and all the Euros, well, they all seemed very European.'

I laughed.

'Pat Cash?' I asked.

'He'd be a towie.'

'A tow truck driver!' I laughed again.

'I'd like to think of him as a tow truck operator – bit like I am,' and he corrected, 'or used to be. Though I never wore a check headband.'

I said I had nothing against tow truck drivers – or operators.

'No offence taken, boy,' said the old bloke with the blue heeler, 'but thanks for the thought.'

I hadn't been called 'boy' for some time and it made me feel a bit odd. Moved. I wondered how old this old bloke with the bluey was.

'He does those hair ads now . . . Pat Cash,' said the red-headed woman.

Nobody said anything.

The man from round the corner asked what John McEnroe would be. 'As well as being a smart alec with a beautiful backhand?' the old bloke replied.

'As well as that,' said the man from round the corner.

'A mathematics teacher, for sure.' The old bloke sighed and then he added, 'You can*not* be serious,' à la McEnroe in his famous screaming rant against an umpire in 1981, and also perhaps to a student who might have come up with the wrong answer to an algebra question.

We were shuffling off in a little clump now, down the sandy track with houses on both sides that leads to the road where we would all disperse to our homes. None of us was in that much of a hurry, we were enjoying the tennis chat and memories, so we all went at the same pace as the blue heeler.

'Still haven't sold that place,' said somebody, referring to a house that had been on the market for a while, and we walked along.

'Who was your favourite player?' asked the red-headed woman to the heeler's owner.

'Newk,' he answered simply.

'Oh, John Newcombe,' the red-haired woman said.

'Yup, Newk,' said the old bloke.

John Newcombe. A tennis titan from the past, but as soon as I heard the name I thought: Kooyong, Cinzano and Norm. And I smiled. Nobody spoke for a moment, but I think we all had the same thought.

The bloke from round the corner said simply, 'Chin-chin.'

I answered, 'Must be the drink for today!'

'Oh my God!' The red-headed woman laughed her nice laugh. 'That ad with Newk and his mo, for Cinzano.'

John Newcombe was a seven-times major singles title winner with a laid-back manner and an iconic handlebar moustache. He was confident, charming and strangely charismatic in a wooden blokey way, with a measured and almost toneless way of speaking that made him pretty loveable. And he seemed to be flogging almost anything.

Some of the ads he was involved in entered the national lingo. The 'Life be in it' campaign, which ran for years, was supposed to inspire Australians to become more physically active, but the major takeaway was that the animated character of Norm, a lazy obese man who was forever sitting in front of his telly with a beer resting on his stomach, was keeping fit by watching the tennis on the TV.

At the end of the ad, he raises his can of beer at the set and mumbles, 'Bewdy, Newk'. So popular was the ad that 'Bewdy, Newk' came to signify someone having a go and doing something positive.

And the same for the Italian vermouth Cinzano, which was flogged by Newk in an ad where he famously talked to the camera and said in that odd voice, 'When I was in Rome, I discovered this great new drink.' The fact that he sounded like your next-door neighbour or the fellow who ran the newsagent made the whole thing delightful. What on earth were people like that doing in Rome? Newk made Rome sound like Chermside. Especially when he delivered the tagline for the ad: 'Must be the drink for today.' He beamed his great white-toothed smile from under his bushy 'tache, and added, 'Chin-chin!'

'It's so modern even a jetsetter like Newk drinks it!' I remember a friend of my mother's saying at a barbecue as she brandished a bottle.

'Yeah,' said the old bloke, 'Newk would sell his shadow if there was coin in it. Good on him. He was a bloke, no angles to him.'

'I remember the ads more than him playing,' said the red-headed woman.

'I can remember the '73 Davis Cup win, five zip,' said the man from round the corner. 'And that Christmas I got a K-tel album with John Newcombe talking about tennis.'

I said I vaguely remembered this and then I clicked my fingers to help me think. The old bluey turned his pop-eyed head and gave a muffled bark, an old dog's bark.

'Shush up, Wally, it's not time for food.' The old man explained that when he was ready to feed the old bluey – Wally – he would click his fingers. 'Poor old Wal is half blind, but he gets about.'

'Sorry, Wal,' I said and bent down and gave him a pat. 'I can remember, Newk' – nobody was calling him John Newcombe; it was nickname only – 'beating Connors at Kooyong. Newk had a wooden racquet and Jimmy Connors' was metal.'

'And then the next year he got done in the final by the hospital janitor. Mark Edmondson,' said the red-headed woman.

It was true: a rank outsider, Mark Edmondson had been working as a hospital janitor just two weeks before the Australian Open of that year.

'Kooyong!' continued the red-headed woman. 'My sister went to see the Rolling Stones there. It was so hot, and she got so sunburnt. And my father couldn't get over how Newk won the Open that year and a couple of weeks later, all these long-haired yahoos – that's what he called the Rolling Stones, yahoos – were playing "that rock and roll rubbish!"'

The old bloke nodded. 'I went to that concert, didn't get sunburnt, the night-time show, but it was awfully hot. My thirtieth birthday present from my wife.'

'Did she go?' asked the red-headed woman.

'The Red-Headed Woman' sounded like a song the Stones would sing.

The old bloke nodded. 'Married fifty years.' He looked off down the street and said matter-of-factly, 'Miss her.'

Nobody asked what had happened. I think we all just assumed she had died. The old man took a bit of a breath. 'Long-haired yahoos – we were all like that, I reckon, even Newk.' He looked back at us. 'And he always had a go, Newk, never shirked. You know why he was my favourite?'

We all waited. Even Wally seemed interested. 'After a fault, his second serve was nearly always harder than the first. Only player I've ever seen do that.'

We were at the end of the track and that meant the end of the chat. We all stood and then the old man said, softly, 'Bewdy, Newk.'

He clicked his fingers and he and Wally shuffled off together.

'I'm going to look for that Newk album,' said the man from round the corner. 'Pretty sure it's in the shed somewhere.' And he laughed. 'That's the sort of stupid thing you do this time of the year, isn't it? Hunt through the shed trying to find a memory.' And he nodded and walked off.

The red-headed woman and I said goodbye, and I thought about that concert at Kooyong on that hot summer night, the old man's thirtieth birthday present from his wife of fifty years. I supposed his wife had only died a few years ago.

I watched the old man and his old blue heeler walking away. It was just a chat about the tennis on the beach with people from the neighbourhood, but it seemed like a little more.

And for the old man, for the wife he missed and for Wally, and maybe for the red-headed woman, her sunburnt sister and the bloke searching in his shed for a memory, I offered up to the afternoon words that seemed quite apt. 'Bewdy, Newk.'

Then I walked home.

•

When I used to live in the city, during this fallow time of the year when the tennis ruled, you'd see people who looked and dressed a little differently: tennis tourists. They weren't in any way offensive or unpleasant; indeed there was an air of politeness and good humour to them. They were simply different.

Like some offshoot species of human evolution, they were very neatly dressed and usually had American or European accents – which sounded oddly the same – and always had their shirts tucked in their pants so tightly I wondered if they had used industrial adhesive or rivets to secure the two garments. There was hardly any wrinkle to be seen, everything seemed very straight and correct. Their voices were a little louder, very clearly articulated and they didn't walk so much as slowly parade and survey, going at their own pace.

Apparel, apparently, was what they wore. Sporting apparel, mostly tennis apparel, but certainly all apparel could be comfortably labelled sporting apparel. So, I called them Apparelists.

What is the difference between sporting apparel and clothes you wear when you actually play sport? The easy answer is that you sweat and strain with endeavour in sportswear but in sports apparel you stroll about with an entitled air with whatever brand and brand slogan you think befits your character.

Just do it. All in. Impossible is nothing. Forever faster. My time is now. On and on go the slogans.

Once my local tennis club decided to hold a weekend tournament just prior to the start of the Australian Open. On the club's noticeboard was a flyer for the 'event'. It was rather hopefully and ambitiously called 'A Celebration of Tennis'.

A mate was enthusiastic, I was less so. 'Come on, Will, why don't you give it a crack before your knees completely give out on you?'

'You just want someone you know you can beat there,' I replied.

This was no theory, it was fact. After way too much wear and tear from all the sport I'd played during my life, the cartilage in my knees was a distant and almost fading memory. If my very social style of tennis could be described, it would be defined as 'oil rig baseline'. I had no lateral movement, and the idea of serve and volleying was never going to be considered. I could serve and if the ball was near, I could thump it back.

One of the other members called me 'the Death Star' after the Star Wars' intergalactic hardware – you know, Darth Vader's cubbyhouse. Her exact words were, 'You're like a great big orb that doesn't move much but could emit the occasional bit of destruction – just like the Death Star.'

My friend nodded. 'Yes, mate. I won't deny that I would feel more comfortable having somebody I know I can trounce, but it'll be a bit of fun.'

I said okay, and had another drink.

Another friend, who wasn't interested in playing, offered to 'caddy' for us because it might be funny.

'It's not golf, you clown,' I said, 'it's tennis.'

'Oh, spot on. Listen, I'll be like your squire, the second to you two noble knights engaging in a bit of racquet jousting.'

What could go wrong?

My playing mate, who our squire dubbed Sir Toby because his name was Toby, had visions of a couple of sets of genteel, good-humoured tennis followed by a visit to the clubhouse for a refreshing Pimm's and the occasional cucumber sand-wich. Me? I was looking forward to a Vic Bitter and a packet of chips.

'Oh, you are all class, Sir Orb,' said our squire.

Sir Toby called me a boofhead, to which I retorted, 'I live in the real world, old cock, no Pimm's south of the equator.'

'I stand with Sir Orb,' said our squire.

Sir Toby said he was just getting into the spirit of things and that was why he was wearing his Nike shirt, with 'Just Do It' printed on his chest.

'It's a knock-off from a market in Da Nang, but I want to look the part.'

'Toby Da Nang,' I said, rolling the name around in my mouth. 'It sounds like a US top tenner from the nineties.'

'I'll take that,' said Sir Toby Da Nang. Looking the part.

On the day of the tournament, I was wearing Ruggers shorts and a Father's Day present from my youngest, a comfy, flowing fishing shirt from an outdoor chain that had a great gaping-mouthed fish on it. I don't know if it was in any way tennis apparel but that was what I was wearing.

When I saw who had turned up to compete, I had the distinct impression that I wasn't anywhere within even half a trick of pulling whatever it was I was trying to pull off.

There were only a few entrants. A round robin was hastily organised. Five in a group, winner to play the final. I looked at my opposition. Poor old Sir Toby wasn't drawn in my group. There was no one who was born when Borg played McEnroe in the comp, save for me and my mate, and definitely nobody who had any idea who Newk was or knew anything about the great drink he discovered in Rome.

My first set was against Kev.

Kev had an entourage: four people who looked just like him. Even the woman who was there looked like Kev. They all wore orange fluoro outfits and Kev's cap had a big K printed on the peak.

'You bring your tribe?' I asked when we shook hands.

'They are my people,' he said.

All I had was my squire, who was severely hungover and shaking. Kev had an esky full of sports drinks; I had a water bottle that my caddy occasionally filled from the clubhouse tap. Kev had a four-tennis-racquet-sized bag, to accommodate his four racquets, each strung at different pressures, depending on the prevailing barometric conditions. I had a racquet that I had used when Kevin Rudd was prime minister the first time around and another piece of equipment that I liked to think of as a novelty secret weapon. It was in a plastic shopping bag.

During warm-up, I mis-hit a couple. That was weird. I actually felt a little nervous. An old rugby coach would sometimes encourage us to have a can of beer – never a stubby because, in his words, 'No matter how careful you are with glass in a change room there will always be breakage' – before a game, 'for the nerves, boys.'

He was also a raging drinker who was seemingly chilled out twenty-four hours a day, so what nerves he had to deal with was anybody's guess but he always enthusiastically joined in with having 'the coldie to combat the jitters'.

I thought I could have done with such a coldie, but then again, I had been out the previous night with my caddy-cum-squire and fellow knight and consumed more than was needed for nerves, or any other reason. A couple of mistimed returns to the corners had Kev saying, 'I hope you aren't going to make me run all day!' How prescient of him. After losing eight quick points and 0–2 done, I offered, 'No, Kev, I don't think I am going to make you run all day. Laugh, yes, snicker possibly but run . . . no.'

I hit a couple of aces and a few winners but Kev soon worked out my limitations and even though 'his people' looked like a cult they turned out to be his family and were just having a bit of fun. They all had the same orange Puma shirts on and K caps and when Kev hit one of his many winners, they held up individual signs that spelt his name. They'd gone to a bit of trouble and it was nice to be a part of it for a short while.

I soon trudged off with a 0–6 scoreline. Where was my bloody squire?

I fetched my own water from the tap and realised my hand was shaking just as much as the squire's, who had turned up with a pie.

'Is that for me?' I asked.

'No, mate, all mine, I'm struggling. So is Sir Toby.'

'He got done too, huh?' I asked.

'No, he retired. Hamstring soreness.'

'Bullshit!' I laughed.

The squire laughed in return. 'Yeah, what an effort, first set. He was getting his arse kicked by a twelve-year-old and he went the hammy to save embarrassment. He went the Da Nang pang.'

We laughed again and then the squire burnt himself on the pie's innards. 'Oh, I'm struggling.'

Next match, Frank appeared; youngish, no airs nor graces, Ivan Lendl–type cap. We faced off. He was in Adidas armour. Three stripes everywhere. Impossible is Nothing. That was the Adidas tagline.

He didn't groan or grunt and was quite pleasant to play against. He served like a social club member, almost as if he was gently swatting flies, but then returned like an angry Roger Federer crossed with King Kong. Wherever I put 'em, he'd return 'em, with interest, force and backspin. I knew I was cooked.

We laughed a couple of times when arsy shots went our way or shot off like a Tesla rocket gone bung, but he did me like a smoked trout. We shook hands and I thought about giving the next match a miss.

And so, we come to Goran. Ah, Goran. Goran was young and resplendent in fluorescent yellow Asics shoes, which matched his fluorescent yellow Asics socks which matched his fluorescent yellow Asics racquet with fluorescent yellow strings. 'Sound Mind, Sound Body.' That was the Asics tagline, but Goran deported himself in a decidedly fluorescent yellow manner – in other words, like an absolute twerp. He was Goran out of his mind. But that was nothing to do with Asics, that was all Goran.

He was a grunter.

If I last half an hour with him, I thought, I will be either blind or deaf or both. Thankfully, neither eventuated, and I shuffled off the court a short time later, 0–6.

My caddy was there with a water bottle, which he rather unsteadily handed to me. 'Forever faster,' he advised me, quoting the Puma tagline, and then hastened to a seat. I went to open the water bottle and realised there was nothing in it. I pointed this out to the squire and all he said was, 'Oh, I'm really struggling.' I saw he had moved on to a sausage roll. A recovery pie and a recovery sausage roll, yes, he was struggling all right.

One last match in the round robin under an unforgiving summer sun, with an overly dry northerly and I knew I could no longer Just Do It.

I must have looked like the gasping fish on my shirt. I was fairly shot and I turned to my hamstrung Sir Toby and squire. 'Might have to pull the pin,' I declared.

'No, Sir Orb, fight on,' said my squire through mouthfuls of his recovery sausy roll.

Sir Toby of Hamstring spoke, 'No, mate, come on, see it out.' Coming from him that just made me laugh.

'Impossible is nothing' was on Frank's shirt. Impossible is certainly something, I thought, it had been staring me in the face all arvo. Who, I thought, came up with these silly lines? I bet they wouldn't last two minutes in A Celebration of Tennis.

Finally, Finn appeared. There were no Da Nang knock-offs for him; he was head to toe in Just Do It. He was tall, looked very fit and had a face that was impassive, which was topped by a blond buzz cut.

He should have been called Drago because he was almost a spit for the villainous Russian boxer, a character from a wonderful crappy film called *Rocky IV.* 'I must destroy you,' intoned Drago in the movie as the boxers touch gloves.

Finn didn't disappoint. When we shook hands before the match he said, 'I am here to win,' in a monotone and with a steady stare.

'I don't think you'll be disappointed, mate,' I assured him.

'But give me your best,' he said and took up his position to receive my serve.

He was just a person, I thought, just a human, dressed head to toe in Just Do It. What an odd collection of people here at the Celebration of Tennis on courts far removed from Kooyong or the Tennis Centre in Melbourne. What an odd thing to be doing on a hot arvo, being told by Captain Ivan Finn Drago to give him my best.

I stood there and I bounced the ball, and I thought, not Just Do It but more Oh Fuck It! And I gave old Drago my best. I let off a Death Star serve that would have taken out Alderaan from *Star Wars*; a meteor that would have destroyed the dinosaurs. Well, not all of them. I mean I was still around. An Irascible Rex-a-Saurus. It was a killer serve and went the right side of the centre line. I like to think it almost left a skid mark.

'Aye, Sir Orb!' roared the squire.

Finn looked at me with suspicion.

I said to him, 'That was it, son, that was my best and you got it. You'll be right from here.'

And he was. One game down then two then after the third and a change of ends my squire came up to me with a driver he had taken from the set of clubs he had in his boot.

'Here, this might help,' and we both laughed.

The fourth passed into history quicker than the first Pope John Paul, the fifth followed suit.

So, we came to the sixth. Time, I thought, for the novelty secret weapon. I walked over to my shopping bag and, like an old general carefully drawing out an antique sabre from a scabbard, I pulled out a Dunlop wooden racquet, with a glowering John McEnroe with a full head of hair complete with headband in its neck.

I walked back out on the court. The squire said simply, 'A bit of teak!'

Finn Drago stared at me. 'What is that?'

'The past, mate,' I said.

And I went to return his service. It was the best I'd played with my old wooden number. Perhaps Finn Drago couldn't get used to the pace of the strings, the deadened wooden rim shots that arsily landed where they had no right.

But he still cleaned me up. We shook hands.

'Well,' said Finn, 'that was . . . something.'

And he walked off having achieved what he wanted. To win.

I sat with Sir Toby and the squire; they gave me a can of Vic Bitter. After all the tap water I'd sunk during the proceedings I thought I deserved it.

'Oh, the green goblin,' I said, referring to the can of Vic as I cracked it.

'You know, when you got out the old teak racquet,' said the squire, 'it was a bit like Obi-Wan Kenobi pulling out his lightsaber – a definite highlight.'

'Yes, thanks. High praise. I think Obi-Wan Kenobi would be the sort of Jedi Knight to make use of a plastic shopping bag.'

The squire nodded. 'Yes, fits in there snugly, the old lightsaber.'

Sir Toby of Hamstring added, 'I'm going to have to call you Orby-Wan Kenobi.'

We laughed. The day had been a tad embarrassing but it had had its moments.

I thought of all those slogans. Not one fitted aptly, because despite the millions of dollars and hours they spend creating these false hopes, sometimes you just can't do it, sometimes you cannot be forever faster and sometimes it is impossible. And there were no Pimm's and cucumber sandwiches either! But there was an ice-cold Green Goblin and good mates on a sunny summer day.

And it was grand. No slogan needed.

6

BAREFOOT ON BITUMEN

One of the sure signs that you've lived sixty summers is when you look down at your plates of meat. Your feet. An old cricket coach called them 'plates of meat' when he was trying to encourage me to bowl at a fuller length instead of the half-witted short stuff I had been going on with.

'For Christ's sake, you're not quick enough for that sort of palaver, you big drongo. Pitch it up, aim for his plates of meat and you'll give yourself a chance of skittling him.'

My plates of meat. Rhyming slang. My feet.

I usually see them in the morning when I look down as I sit on my bed. It's like saying hello to a pair of old friends. Even that morning when I went for a walk out along the jetty in Busselton, there they were.

Some days, I'll mutter in a matter-of-fact tone to my two noble slabs, 'Hello you.' They never answer back and I suppose that is because they have been through a bit. They look like they have. They have been utterly stoic, taking me wherever I have travelled. And even though the nails look like something from a modernist sculpture gallery and occasionally the rest of the slabs of meat look slightly puffy, all in all they have done the job.

I only say this about feet because, apart from your hands, the feet are the easiest part of your body to see.

Until you catch sight of yourself in the bathroom mirror and see a life journey reflected before you – in my case, a rather corpulent full-blown Spanish galleon of a man – and that sometimes gives me a start. But mostly I give the apparition a cursory glance, occasionally a baleful glare, and I get on with the day.

I spend more time saying hello to my feet.

They have, I admit, had a lot to carry, but what strikes me most about feet is that you see them at a distance. They are not as close as your hands or forearms and one tends to get a sense of perspective when you look down at them.

And that perspective also makes me think of summer. One of the signs of summer that was tangible and visceral was when you'd feel the heat on the soles of your bare feet.

Bare feet used to be all the rage when I was a boy. I spent quite a bit of my primary school years going to and from Humpybong Primary in bare feet.

The trip there and back would give you a whole new sensory adventure because the soles of your feet seemed to suck up the soul of the terrain.

The sharpness of gravel, the plushness of the grass, the footpath's concrete would tell you that the seasons were changing.

In summer it was all you could do to keep your feet on the pavement, it was that hot, and if you ducked down Ella Street to walk along the beach to school, it became fraught with danger because you would have to decide whether you'd risk the minefield of the embedded bindis or hop along the bitumen and kerb and channelling of the road.

Kerb and channelling. How those two words haunted the snatches of conversations overheard between grown-ups for a time in Redcliffe. Progress was coming to the peninsula and Redcliffe was losing its unsealed roads. The walk to school was punctuated by watching graders and concreters change the landscape of the streets with curves of cement added to create a gracious border and better drainage.

I always liked seeing big things being made in public and I remember watching the workers mould and form the channelling, thinking it looked quite lovely.

There was, I recall, a worker in shorts, footy socks and boots, with a check shirt undone almost to his navel. He had a cigarette in one hand and a trowel in the other and he was appraising a bit of formwork for the new guttering. He frowned and sweat beaded on his face. He bent down and gently swept the trowel across the curve of the channelling.

Then he stood up slowly, looked again, stuck his durry in his mouth, inhaled and then blew out a seemingly endless stream of smoke before finally nodding in satisfaction.

He looked over to me. I nodded to him, like I had seen my father do when he was working.

The man with the trowel smiled and then said, 'Yeah, not too bad. Hot work though,' and he winked at me.

The other workers called out to him. 'Hey Pat! Over here.' And he walked over to another piece of formwork.

Many years later I came across the Tate Gallery's collection of Henry Moore sculptures.

The rolling curves of the sculptures seemed to flow as if they were almost breathing. As I looked at the beautiful forms before me, I could almost imagine Henry Moore gently brushing his hands along the lines of what he had created. And I remembered that arvo, walking along Oxley Avenue watching the council workers roll out the kerb and channelling. I felt my feet go all lizardy as if they were back standing in a Queensland summer, and I thought of Pat and his ciggie. His furrowed brow, his deep breath of concentration, the gracious flick of his magic trowel.

I laughed at how incongruous the collision of memory and the art in the gallery felt. Both were beautiful. I wondered if Henry Moore blew out a deep breath of satisfaction with what he had done or if he looked at his work and then said, 'Not too bad.'

I thought of the grown-ups' voices talking about the spreading art of kerb and channelling.

'They've kerb and channelled McDonald Road, any time now they'll come to Oxley Avenue,' said a parent.

'And they've started the kerb and channelling along Landsborough Avenue too,' was the reply.

I heard my Aunty Rita say, 'Too much concrete makes everything so hot in summer, don't you think?'

Me and my bare feet certainly did.

It didn't get any better when you stood at school assembly on the asphalt parade ground while the headmaster droned on, seemingly ignorant of the shifting feet of the multitude of young minds under his academic guidance as we hopped from one foot to another to avoid the soles of our feet melting.

The adventure of an Ella Street trek resembled a wildlife documentary about those great-eyeballed lizards who existed in scorching desert sands and had some odd dance-like movement where they would lift one foot and then another to cool the bottom of their lizardy feet. On Ella Street you'd hop from one foot to another and do the lizardy dance along the gutter of the road, but sometimes it would get a bit too much and so you'd have to risk the bindis.

There were other impediments to the bitumen or guttering route as well: broken bottles or, even worse, the remains of dead cane toads.

The flattened silhouettes were half manageable, they were like the shapes made by the Looney Tunes' Wile E. Coyote when he plummeted through a valley floor after tumbling from a cliff trying to catch the Road Runner, but anything a little fresh or with the residue of what should have been inside the dreadful things now lying outside after coming off second best to a Torana or some other vehicle was beyond the pale.

I whinged to my parents once about how hot my feet got during the summer months and they shared rather scornful looks. 'Well, you can always wear your shoes if you want.'

My shoes. Black leather 'good' shoes or my football boots. I knew I couldn't get away with either. The 'good shoes' were a target for derision and the footy boots were a recent addition to the world of growing up that I was still a little unsure about.

Once you reached double digits you had to play footy in boots and, while I liked playing footy, the idea of encasing your feet in something meant that things were changing; you were growing up. And while I was certainly no Mowgli – the orphaned boy from Kipling's *The Jungle Book* – there was a part of me that liked being a kid who ran around barefooted.

I knew that 'good' shoes and footy boots led the way to sandshoes and gym boots, then those underhand footwear agent 'slippers' that made it seem you had to cover up your feet at night – ancestors perhaps to Dream Socks – then maybe desert boots, runners and tennis shoes and then that was it – you were a grown-up.

Even though I whinged, I liked running and playing and walking barefoot. Loved the way on a hot summer day you did the lizardy dance across the bitumen, then onto the thin grass covered with the fallen scaly bark and fine needles of the pine trees of Suttons Beach, then down the baking cement of the steps and then onto a different heat – the sand.

Then you really were a lizard, skipping across the grains until you got where you desired: into the water. Warm in the shallows and then the delicious cool and almost cold of the deep. Your feet the first to feel it.

I loved all that.

But the outside-insides cane toads' corpses? The bindis? My shoes? Should I?

My father was shocked to think that I was tossing up footwear options.

'Oh, come on,' he said. 'You wouldn't find Tarzan moaning about running around with no shoes! What sort of a King of the Jungle are you?'

This was true. Tarzan wouldn't moan. But he lived in the jungle. I lived in Redcliffe. I didn't want to fight lions, just get to where I was going without burnt feet. And Tarzan swung everywhere on vines, so no need to worry about bindis and burnt feet, just grab a vine and yodel.

Why did he yodel? That was the sound you made when prickles stuck in your soles or your skin blistered.

I couldn't quite see what my father meant. What did Tarzan have to do with me and Humpybong Primary? True, there were some rough nuts at school, but none in loincloths with sharp knives threaded through them.

The old-time Tarzan, Johnny Weissmuller's broken English and small vocabulary made him sound like he'd just come back from a lengthy session at the Mariner's Bar at the Moreton Bay Hotel. 'Tarzan have night on turps but come home with meat tray! Hunt good!'

But Tarzans, like the times, were a-changin'.

They stopped being Jungle Kings and began to look like suburban blokes adrift. The new Tarzan on telly, a man called Ron Ely, looked like he had more oil in his mane than there was in the Middle East.

He had a louche Southern Californian manner that made him sound like he had just come from a Beach Boys recording session. He was so laid-back it looked like he was yawning when he fought the lion in the opening credits.

No, Tarzan in any of his incarnations was a barefoot champ I couldn't hope to compete with.

Though the idea of Tarzan in footy boots or even good shoes did make me smile, especially him running down Ella Street with all the dogs barking and him yodelling and then all the dogs howling in return.

If I was going to wear shoes, which pair would it be?

There was starting to be a definite push from authority for encased feet.

One particular year, as that odd summer highlight of our education came around – school photos – I remember the teacher saying to the class with a general hint of encouragement, 'It's school photos tomorrow, remember to look as neat as you can and it might be an idea to wear shoes . . . of some sort.'

Some kid asked if we had to wear shoes.

The teacher was more pointed in his reply. 'If you want to wear shoes make sure they are your best.' This advice, you must remember, was given with the knowledge that Humpybong Primary was a school in a permanent state of free dress, there wasn't – and had never been – any uniform set for the students. So one could always tell how seriously some families took the whole ritual of the school photo. Hair was plaited or combed, and even on some occasion Brylcreemed. It was a part of Humpybong folklore that some kid always turned up in a tie and no shoes.

Talk about having a bob each way.

I usually rocked up in much the same state as for any school day, namely looking like an unmade bed. A template I have followed for most of my life, much to the dismay of some of those close to me.

Hardly any school kids wore hats of any kind, especially on school photo day – all that neat hair couldn't dare be put out of place – and I'm sure that years down the track there were quite a few dermatologists who did a fair trade because of a lack of sun awareness.

Most kids just wore what they always wore and tried to smile as normally as they could. Or just stared ahead at whoever was taking the photo. 'The Photographer' was his title, like a character, perhaps a baddie, in a Marvel movie franchise. The Photographer was some anonymous grown-up who would pretend to be happy to see us and, in a rather bored tone, would ask us – one year I swore he said 'invite' us – to smile and look natural.

Trying to look natural was a strange idea. What was natural about being herded into a flat-top pyramid of young people standing on thin platforms, and getting a bit embarrassed if you stood too near or too far from the kid next to you?

The resulting image was a collection of sullen-faced, slack-jawed, low-browed beings, a fair few manic closed-eyed grinners, some lovely young faces and the dreaded half-blinkers.

My parents would usually entertain themselves by taking in the recorded image when the day had come to bring it home.

One year – the 'I invite you to look natural' year – my parents pawed the photo. 'Christ alive!' my father almost erupted. 'Look at the boy!'

He was referring to me.

'He looks half normal!'

'I don't believe it! A nice smile and both his eyes are open!' My mother sounded like she had just witnessed the creation of the universe and was genuinely surprised.

This I understood. I had produced a litany of awful school photos. Half-blinks. Vacant stares and crazed grinning glares. One such effort prompted my father to call me Hillbilly Billy. 'You definitely don't look right. Too much moonshine.'

To have produced a 'natural' photo was an achievement.

My parents moved on through the rest of the class. 'Oh, that's the painter's daughter – she looks like her mum . . . which is a pity,' muttered my mother.

'A fair few mugshots-in-waiting there,' offered my father.

'Colin!' yelled my mum.

'I'm just saying. Look – that one is armed burglary for sure, and that lad's bound for Boggo Road for something.' Boggo Road was the notorious prison in Brisbane.

'Is that the youngest Greenwood girl? She's so sweet.'

And my mother would conclude the appraisal as she almost always did with, 'Well, there's a whole life of adventure ahead for all those young faces, God willing, and no bare feet in the front row.'

This second part was for my benefit because when that teacher had told us if we were to wear shoes we should make sure they were our best, I took that to heart. So did another boy. We both packed our best shoes and when it was time for the class to gather and The Photographer went through his preamble, my classmate and I had quickly put on our best shoes.

The Photographer was going to say something about being natural when he stopped and then stared as we stood at the back of the assembled class.

'What are you two boys wearing?' he said.

The teacher looked over and then both he and The Photographer laughed.

'That's a first, two boys in football boots for a class photo.' The Photographer smiled.

'I did say their best shoes,' said the teacher.

Not our 'good' shoes, but our best. The other boy's were a pair of Gola boots and mine came from Kmart.

Our mums heard about our footwear while on tuckshop duty and my mum was waiting for me at the big dining table that arvo. She told me to sit down. She asked how my radials were. 'Radials' was the word my parents began using to describe my feet after my complaints about the summer heat on the footpaths.

'Look, you, look here,' she said as she gently tapped the back of my head.

She had made a Milo and some Vegemite toast for me and had put the treats in front of me. She held up class photos of my siblings and one of mine.

'Look at the front row. All girls and all wearing shoes or sandals. And what do you see at the back? Hardly any legs, is there? And I bet you they are all barefooted Tarzans!'

She was right. All the front row were girls, the ones who had taken the photo seriously, seriously enough to have neat hair, made an effort with the clothes, smiled nicely and all sat with their hands tucked into their laps for modesty's sake, as suggested by The Photographer. 'Hands in your laps, girls. Just to be safe!' he had said. I don't think any of us kids knew what on earth he meant by that, just an idiosyncrasy of The Photographer.

And the rest of us stood behind them, legs and feet hidden behind the selected front row. I needn't have worried about my best shoes.

My mother laughed as she saw the realisation dawn on me as I picked up my cold Milo. Then she looked at the photos.

'All those young faces,' she said as I sipped my Milo, and she gently and almost absently stroked the back of my head.

I wonder if The Photographer ever thought one face had stood out from all those young faces he had organised into position. Had there been one that had caught his attention, perhaps a few he had remembered?

It was quite a privilege to record a moment in time of someone's life. Back then a photograph was more than just the pushing of a button on an iPhone or Android, a whole stream of digitally recorded pixels collecting among the device's data.

I wonder if The Photographer had a favourite photo that he took. And I wonder if anybody else had worn their footy boots. Their best shoes.

•

After the 'best shoes' incident my mother decided it was time for a trip to Wimberley's to sort out my cream-bun Tarzan feet. Meaning they were soft. This trip sealed the summer foot style for good. It was time, she said, that I had a proper pair of thongs.

Off to Wimberley's, one of the two shoe shops in Redcliffe. The other was a Mathers store. People either went to one or the other, sometimes both, but everyone was shy of letting the staff of either shop know where they had been. It was nothing to see the children of some parent who had gone to Wimberley's sitting just outside the shop with Mathers bags and vice versa.

But Redcliffe being Redcliffe, everybody knew where everybody had been, so it was a pointless if polite exercise.

Mathers was a successful chain from Brisbane and was the flashier outfit, as 'boutique', if you like, as Redcliffe could get. It was run by a very neat, natty and 'theatrical' manager. Amongst his employees was a natty, neat and not-so-theatrical young assistant with red hair who could be quite flamboyant if he wanted to sell a particular pair of shoes.

When I was a teenager I tried to make some half-arsed joke I had heard at footy training about Mathers being the place where you'd buy fancy shoes.

At footy the backs were sometimes called Tinkerbells, after the gamine fairy from *Peter Pan* because they weren't in the thick of it like the forwards who blundered around doing all the grunt work in the engine room. No, the backs were where fairies dusted the shoulders of the players and anything could happen.

A winger was always prone to derision, especially so when he was a red-haired blood nut who had a habit of running with the ball before he had properly caught it, as if he never really wanted to catch the bloody thing in the first place.

'He looks like he's trying to catch a hot kettle off the stove,' was my Aunty Rita's opinion of the blood nut's ball-handling skills.

Poor blood nut would jiggle as he juggled the ball, then he'd stop still to balance himself, then secure the hot kettle and race off again. With so many moving parts something was bound to go wrong, and he had a tendency to stumble and trip over himself. So one training session some wag had said, 'Hey, Tinkerbell. Did you buy your boots from Mathers?'

Then at a family barbecue my Aunty Rita said she was going to come in during the week and get some nice new dress shoes. Meaning she'd come in from the sticks to Redcliffe to a 'good' shop.

I tried to riff on the winger sledge and suggested she try Mathers because that was where the fairy godmother and Tinkerbell shopped.

My Old Man pulled me up. 'If you're trying to be funny, shut your trap. They are good blokes who earn an honest living. They don't deserve smart-arseness like that. And I don't mind buying my good shoes from there.'

My mother and aunt laughed. 'When do you buy good shoes?'

'Well, if I did, I'd shop there. Good blokes.' And he paused. 'Tinkerbell told me.'

We laughed.

He came up to me and gently punched my arm. 'You're all right, but don't talk like a goose. They are good blokes. They're who they are. Nothing wrong with that. You just remember that.'

I nodded. My Old Man could be as mad as a cut snake and epically incorrect but in his core was an astoundingly good and decent man.

So, despite the odd dip into the exotic world of the Mathers shoe shop, we were definitely a Wimberley's family.

Wimberley's was a family affair run by Redcliffe locals. Mr Wimberley, instead of being neat and natty, always gave the air of being very crisp, as if he had just showered. He was very polite, bordering on dour, and was described by a friend of my father's with these words: 'I think he crosses himself the right way but he runs that shop like a Presbyterian. Good value to be had.'

Many years later, Mr Wimberley ran for mayor but didn't quite get enough votes even though he was a highly regarded Redcliffe citizen. My Aunty Rita had a theory on his lack of political success. 'Well, I think he's seen too many people's feet. They can be dreadful things, feet – fallen arches, thickened nails, lumps, corns, sprains, gout and goodness knows what. He's been too close to what people have tried to hide; he's seen too many secrets that lie under a boot's leather for them to vote for him!'

Anyway, he was a lovely man and he had a lovely shop.

Wimberley's had a tiled entrance and on either side were large rectangular display windows where the stock was featured, sometimes on wedges to give the shoes an appealing angle.

Occasionally, encased in some shoes would be a mannequin's ankle and foot, giving the impression of some awful traumatic accident. As if some dreadful act of dismemberment had taken place and all these amputated feet were left wearing shoes.

My sense of summer changed when Mr Wimberley, after greeting my mother, sat me down and placed my foot on a metal measuring plate. Being measured for a pair of thongs. Surely an indication of a time past.

I looked down at my feet on the plate. The same sort of view from my bed now, only my plates of meat had yet to carry me through six decades. The silence was broken by Mr Wimberley. He said, 'Your second toe is longer than your big toe.'

Was this something to be worried about? A grown-up pronouncing judgement on my feet?

'A sign of intelligence and beauty,' said my mother.

Mr Wimberley nodded. 'Some people do indeed say that. I've heard the ancient Greeks said it can be a sign of physical perfection and other people say it's also a sign of a bad temper. But to me,' he looked up and smiled, 'it means you've got to have a comfortable fit. Even in thongs.'

Mr Wimberley knew his feet. Having your second toe longer than the big toe wasn't that rare, apparently, and it comes along with a number of names: Morton's toe, Viking toe, royal toe and turkey toe. I was hoping for a Tarzan amongst the toe titles but apparently it wasn't there.

Mr Wimberley brought over a pair of black rubber thongs, size 6. He laid them before me, took away the measuring plate and slipped them on my feet.

'They are double-plugged,' he said, as if that would impress me.

'Where are they from?' I heard myself ask.

'Oh, well,' Mr Wimberley took a breath. 'They've been around for years one way or another. Some say the Ancient Egyptians wore thongs, and Indians, but I think the Japanese popularised them. Geishas used to wear them.'

'I know his second toe is longer than the big one,' my mother said, 'but I hope you're not saying the boy is a geisha prospect?'

Mr Wimberley played that one with a straight bat. 'No, of course not. Far from it. No need for foot binding. Just trying to give some history to the footwear.'

'Where are they made?' I said slowly.

Mr Wimberley looked at me. 'Here. In Australia. Dunlop. Top quality. And they are double-plugged.' And he nodded.

I walked with them, a little unsteadily but not disliking the sensation.

Thongs. Are they even called that now?

Australians were first introduced en masse to thongs in the late fifties and early sixties when Dunlop began manufacturing hundreds of thousands of them here. They were casual, cheap and comfortable.

And popular. So popular, they became thought of as an iconic part of Australian dress.

But popularity bred contempt and before long thongs were banned from worksites and workplaces for safety concerns. In 1978 the Queensland Government banned the wearing of thongs at Australian Citizenship ceremonies because they wanted to add a bit more sartorial dignity to the whole occasion.

Hard to believe that wearing something that was such a part of the national character would be outlawed when somebody took up the nationality of their new country.

I was bewildered to discover there were so many other names for thongs. Flip flops, scuffs. In India thongs are known as *chappals*. In Latin America they are *chanclas*, in the Bahamas thongs are known as 'slippers' and of course there is the New Zealand term 'jandal'. A mix of Japanese and sandals.

An old bloke who drank at the Crab Pot bar at the Ambassador Hotel on Marine Parade referred to his thongs as his 'dancing shoes' or his 'Fred and Gingers' after the cinematic dancing couple Fred Astaire and Ginger Rogers. He would perch on a tall bar stool and tap along with his thongs flapping in beat to the music from a jukebox in the corner.

The casual nature of thongs led to variations on a theme: the deeply loved but widely loathed Crocs, a byproduct of some petrochemical laboratory, which my mother called 'formal thongs'. Even the ridiculous Dr Scholl health sandal, the wooden ones with supposed arch support and the massage sandals that had the soles covered with tiny hard rubber bollards that were designed to give relief and comfort to the wearer but were really just a form of torture inspired by the Spanish Inquisition.

These things were passed off as casual summer wear.

And of course the Birkenstock, a German sandal and half shoe made from moulded layers of cork. The Volvo of footwear costs a bomb and looks like a box. I once saw a television director of infinite intelligence wearing a pair of open-toed Birkenstocks on location in Darwin and his feet, epically flat and rather prehistoric, gave me a hint of the possibility of the devolution of modern man back to a Fred Flintstone era.

To many people a thong isn't even a piece of footwear, it's a type of undergarment or swimming costume.

It's there when you type 'thongs' into a search engine. True, there are a few images of rubber footwear but then a multitude of other thong things appear, most of them designed to be worn between the cheeks of your bum.

This incarnation of a thong, when added to the concept of double-plugging, makes the mind boggle.

Double-plugging sounded almost as mystical as kerb and channelling.

Thongs, of the footwear variety, could elicit unexpected responses and could be used to provoke one of my father's many colourful phrases to describe someone lacking a bit of smarts.

'Christ, he is so stupid that bloke in the Seabrae bottle-o, he can never give the right change – so stupid, he doesn't know how to tie up his thongs.'

Were they supposed to have laces, I wondered. Was that a problem? I decided to ask my Old Man.

He looked at me, took a breath, shook his head then attempted to explain, but ended up giving me a pre-emptive bit of character assessment.

'Christ, boy, how many times were you dropped on your head? Thongs don't have laces, but that bugger is so dumb he thinks they should have 'em. They are not there, but he still thinks he has to try to tie 'em up. He is that stupid. Do you get me, boy?'

I just stared and my father sighed, then patted me on the head. 'Oh, you're all right.'

When I looked at my new thongs, I suddenly understood what my father had meant. I nodded to myself and when I showed them off to my father I said, 'No laces.'

He looked at me for a moment, and I thought he was going to ask again how many times I'd been dropped on my head, but instead he laughed and patted me on my back as if I had reached some pivotal milestone in life. 'Well done, boy! Your first pair of Malayan Slappers.'

Malayan Slappers was his term for thongs, based on the assumption that Malayan rubber was what the things were constructed from. His original term had been Malayan Rubber Slappers, from the slapping sound the rubber made against your feet – but my mother had objected to how that sounded and so he used Malayan Slappers instead and somehow this was deemed more polite. In time it got downstreamed to merely 'Slappers' but it still made my mother wince slightly.

And he nodded, patted me on the head again, then whistled for the dogs to join him to walk the estate.

I looked down at the thong rubber between my big toe and my turkey, Viking, royal, Greek and Morton's second toe. It rubbed a little, but the more I walked in them the more it settled down. That rather spongy piece of rubber – double-plugged for extra strength – felt quite pleasant.

No need to fear the bitumen or the parade ground, no need to worry about bindis. No need to dread the kerb and channelling and the inside-outsides cane toads.

It didn't mean my feet would be impervious to pain wearing thongs. You certainly knew about pain when the front of the base of your thong peeled under itself and you stubbed your toe – and on a bad day, toes – on the hard floor beneath.

Or when you slipped and skimmed on wet concrete, and went arse over tit: that was humiliation and a bump on the coccyx.

The Age of Thongs had begun and it led to all those other forms of summer footwear. Deep within me I knew that my feet were now to be separated from terra firma and the summer heat. The sensation of my feet being cushioned on a warm flap of rubber became a sure sign of summer.

The age of being barefoot had passed.

7

TOGS

Togs, swimmers, cozzies, bathers are so much easier for blokes. Take my father, he just wore a pair of footy shorts – baggy, comfy and handy. And he always insisted on calling them 'trunks', even though when he wore them in the garden or out and about, they were 'footy strides'.

If you attempted to point this out to him, he would look, sniff and call you a 'banjo player' – which was a term he used to describe somebody he thought was an idiot.

'Trunks' must have derived from the literal purpose of the early swimming trunks: to cover the trunk of your body. The only other person I ever heard use the term 'swimming trunks' was a seriously odd physical education teacher we had for half a term who looked like he had stepped out of a P. G. Wodehouse story. He had a handlebar moustache that I think he used to wax, and a whistle which he loved blowing just before he would shriek, 'Swimming trunks, swimming trunks, into your swimming trunks, lads!'

At least my father only said trunks and had no whistle. And instead of shrieking he quite happily roared.

When he wanted to go for a swim and was impatient with other members of the family who might be faffing around, he'd bellow, 'Hurry up and get into your bloody trunks, you banjo players.'

One morning he roared out this advice.

'Oh, Colin!' my mother roared back.

'What?' he bellowed back.

The dogs began to bark, thinking people yelling meant a game or the possibility of getting a feed.

'You sound like some demented ringmaster telling his little people to get into their suitcase!' yelled my mother.

I thought once again of the Yugoslavian acrobatic team.

My father tried to make a bit of sense of my mother's words. He thought for a moment and then shouted, 'Is that from that Charlton Heston circus movie? The one where Jimmy Stewart is the clown?'

The dogs were leaping and barking.

My mother's voice boomed from upstairs. 'The one where he's a doctor on the run from the police?'

'Yes!'

'I have no idea but stop shouting about people getting in their trunks,' shouted my mother as she came down the stairs in her weightlifter's outfit.

'Oh, be quiet!' she advised the dogs with a cry.

The dogs were quiet.

A moment's pause.

Then my father roared, 'Hurry up then and get into your Charlton Hestons!'

The dogs started to leap and bark again, almost as if celebrating the new word for summer swimwear – Charlton Hestons!

It's worse for women, of course. Every spring all the magazines my sisters used to read, like *Cosmopolitan*, *Cleo*, *Vogue* and *Dolly* had advice on just what you needed for new summer fashion. Even the *Courier-Mail*, the fusty and matronly daily Brisbane newspaper, would herald the summer with a picture of what 'we'll be wearing' on the beaches in the coming summer. The 'we' was slightly subjective because of course the photo was of a young woman in a bikini or a one-piece. No need to see a bloke in his 'trunks' alongside as it was taken for granted that's what the other part of 'we' would be wearing.

The fashion spreads were all bent to one end: emptying your pocket to purchase the latest trend. If you didn't want to fork out your money there was always the mug's last chance – the dreaded sewing patterns.

These things – a collection of designs printed on thin tissue paper for articles of clothing which could be traced or cut and then sewn together – came in rectangular packets. On the front were drawn figures in exaggerated poses showing off what the finished garments were supposed to look like. These figures bore no resemblance to a real person – they were thin with exaggerated hair and almond-shaped eyes and looked a little like the sketch illustration underwear advertisements that were always in the *Courier-Mail* on a Wednesday.

'Seriously, the only sort of creature who would wear something like that is one of these funny drawings,' muttered my mother flicking through the *Courier* on the Wednesday morning.

A different adventure, being a woman.

Whenever one of these sewing pattern packets arrived in the house the tension levels would rise exponentially. As soon as the sewing pattern – be it a McCall's, Butterick or the ironically named 'Simplicity' – was plonked down on the big downstairs table where we gathered for meals and debate, the drama began.

Everybody seemed to know, even the dogs and the cat, that a grand undertaking was about to begin; an event which every breathing being within the walls had to live through. Sometimes it was a dress, sometimes a pair of pants, and on one epic occasion a pants suit which my mother tried to make for herself for a Christmas 'social', which in her own words ended up looking like a 'bloody floral straitjacket'.

But for the sheer awful panic, nothing compared to the sewing-kit 'bathing suits'.

Bathing suits, another oddly quaint and formal term for togs, bathers, cozzies, swimmers, trunks and Charlton Hestons.

These sewing kits, the writing on the packet proclaimed, were complete with 'e-z-to-follow instructions' and when they were spread out across the table, they were stared at with eyes that had seen the history of such endeavours.

A little like later generations looking at IKEA instructions to assemble a bookcase or shelving unit. It was Sanskrit essentially, and almost impenetrable.

My sisters had all done Home Economics at high school, had all sat through classes where you cut, joined and stitched pieces of material together, but these lessons were probably the equivalent of my manual training efforts, where attempts to glue and screw bits of wood and metal always ended up in the bin.

My mum could sew and stitch and repair and was a dab hand at fancy dress but there was something about these sewing-kit patterns which would defeat people.

It never deterred the women in my family from trying.

My mother, and whichever sister it was who wanted to make the article of clothing, stared down intensely at the plans before them. Sometimes they were joined by other members of the family.

On the occasion of the 'bathing suit' I went to join the viewing but was stopped at the French doors by my father, who uttered a bit of advice. 'I wouldn't go in there, boy, it's like a cross between someone planning a bank robbery or Eisenhower planning for D-day.'

My mother called any attempts to make sewing patterns into actual garments 'Melanies'. This was after the harrowing scene in one of her favourite films, *Gone with the Wind*, where the character of Melanie, a sickly but sweet Southern lady undergoes the traumatic birth of her child as the Yankees of the North bombard Atlanta.

I never quite knew why the Yankees were supposed to be the baddies if they were fighting for the abolition of slavery, but my mother would always shush anybody who tried to raise the point.

'It's not about slavery, it's about lovely old Big Ears,' meaning the movie's heart-throb, Clark Gable.

One thing I did know was my mother didn't like the character of Melanie Wilkes, who she thought was a 'goody-two-shoes snob'.

During this childbirth scene, there are agonised whispers, yells, silhouettes and high drama amidst the siege at the height of the sweltering humid summer. Goody-two-shoes Melanie whispers lines like 'I'm sorry to be such a bother, Scarlett,' and is a writhing picture of self-sacrifice and stoicism.

I only sat through this movie once with my mother. But as this scene was played out and Melanie Melanie-ed away, my mother muttered, 'What a lot of carry-on, she should try having five of the bloody things.'

It took me a moment, but I realised that the 'things' she was referring to were we five children.

And this traumatic operatic scene was what my mother likened the creation of sewing-kit garments to, and she shared it with her daughters. There was a line uttered by Vivien Leigh's Scarlett O'Hara, 'Don't try to be brave. Yell, Melanie, yell all you want – there's nobody to hear.'

We could all hear.

This advice was taken to heart by my mother, especially when, on an agonisingly humid early summer weekend she and her youngest daughter were trying to make a mission-brown bikini, with the 'fashion feature' bit of the garment being the upper half connected by a circular piece of plastic at the front.

The plastic circle didn't come with the pack, but my sister and mother thought they could use a plastic curtain ring. This entertained my mother because of yet another *Gone with the Wind* reference after a destitute Scarlett O'Hara, dressed in a homemade gown made from curtain fabric, wins the heart of old Big Ears.

Yet it was the earlier *GWTW* reference of yelling 'all you want' which soon became apparent.

'Oh, good God, this is such a bloody Melanie!' bellowed my mother.

'How is D–day coming along, Ike?' asked my father in a pleasant enough tone.

'Be quiet, Colin! Eisenhower never had to try to thread elastic through a seam this tight!'

The image of one of the great military figures of the twentieth century, the wise and affable Dwight D. Eisenhower, losing his rag over a sewing-kit bikini is very hard to shake, once imagined.

The fact that the pattern was from the Simplicity brand only added to the whole opera. 'Simplicity? Bugger off. Why is it they can put a man on the Moon but can't explain how you cross-stitch a French seam? Simplicity! Balls!'

When the thing was finally finished and my sister tried to wear it, everything that was supposed to be inside the mission-brown material had a way of finding its way outside of it, and the curtain ring didn't help.

'I think this might be a backyard job only,' was my sister's curt assessment.

It wasn't only my family that had trouble with sewing kits. Years later at a dinner party, our after-dinner talk found its way on to the subject of what was worn at school formals. A friend said she was determined to wear a gown she had bought the pattern for, and her mother had tried to make it according to the instruction on the packet.

'If I leant my shoulder to the left, it would stay on but if I stood normally it would end up around my feet. But I quite liked it.'

Her father asked why she was walking 'that way' when she was about to leave the house with her partner.

'What way?' my friend replied.

'Like you are off to play *Richard the Third*,' said her father.

Not even the reference to the great hunchback Shakespearean villain could dissuade her from her gown, so well done her.

I couldn't help but ask if she had ever had any swimsuit sewing-kit adventures and she erupted in laughter.

'Swimsuit patterns,' she paused, clapping her hands. 'Now that takes me back.'

She worked in finance and had a unique and quite graphic take on one of her watery efforts. 'Those crocheted bikinis were all the go, and I got a pattern for this string thing.' There was a chorus of groans at the mention of crocheted bikinis.

Somebody said, 'All those little bits of pinprick sunburn you'd get where the weave left little holes!'

My friend went on. 'The kit recommended you use cotton thread, but I thought I'd save money by using my mum's acrylic wool leftovers. So, that one's on me.' She raised her hand in admission of guilt. 'I wore it once, this multicoloured spider's web of a thing — it just soaked up all the water and when I tried to get out, the bloody thing fell faster than the Dow Jones on Black Monday!'

Black Monday was when a financial crisis hit world markets in 1987, and the Dow Jones Index fell a calamitous 22 per cent in one trading session.

•

Just because the Charlton Hestons women wore were a little more complex didn't mean that blokes, even if their beach attire was a bit more basic, didn't have a serious rap sheet when it came to bather crimes.

Take me, for instance. After moving on from my tartan-check numbers I eased into fluctuating between the inspired Budgie Smugglers, Ruggers footy shorts and the occasional pair of board shorts.

I can't quite remember who bought my Stubbies board shorts but when I received the gift, I thought I had at last cracked it in the fashion stakes. These were brand-name daks – so deluded was I that I actually thought Stubbies products were something to be proud of.

Stubbies shorts, infamous in their ill-fitting crotch and silly dinky little pocket just above the right thigh at hip height. The board shorts were no better and probably took the design faults into niche territory. In fact, when thinking about great design faults, you could go so far as to say that if those Stubbies board shorts were a soft drink they would undoubtedly be New Coke. If they were an automobile they would undoubtedly be a Leyland P76. And if those Stubbies board shorts were a hairstyle they would undoubtedly be a permed mullet.

They were that bad.

They were banana-yellow in colour and had white piping around the bottom hem. The late seventies and early eighties had a lot to answer for in terms of sartorial body-hugging oddness.

And if those board shorts didn't glow in the dark then they should have for they had a vaguely contaminated radioactive look as well as being very short and very tight. Added to this was the fact that these board shorts had the famous Stubbies crotch, or rather the non-crotch, which added a new dimension to compartmentalisation in clothing.

My whole nether regions looked like some stop-animation relief model from a social studies documentary about changing urban sprawl because everything was dispersed and then pushed into a clumping bunch. Then, after bunching, they would disperse and bunch together on the other side of the crotch seam.

I was slightly aware of this whole process, but somehow in my burgeoning adolescent brain I thought it might be how the Banana Chunder Boardies functioned. And anything that could draw attention to my meat and two veg was at least a talking point that could lead to further adventures. Or so I thought.

In any case, people weren't shy in coming forward with opinions.

I should have quickly worked out that those board shorts weren't the go, but sometimes you have to be hit over the head with the truth even after a couple of good hints.

One summer Saturday mid arvo, mooching through Redcliffe's shops after sport, I grabbed a chocolate thickshake and headed off to one of my favourite peninsula haunts – the Record Market in Sutton Street.

It was one of a chain of shops across south-east Queensland, but in the days before the internet and streaming, it felt like a conduit to the world – all the latest music arriving not long after you'd seen it on *Countdown*, the national pop music show on the fusty old ABC on a Sunday early evening.

The Record Market didn't have all the tripe that was in Kmart or Chandlers, the reissues of your parents' music like Percy Faith and Mantovani that even they thought was rubbish. And if the Record Market had compilations, it wasn't the TV specials like panpipes playing movie themes; it was the gold-plated K-tel stuff such as *Ripsnorter* and *Full Boar* or *Soul* collections. Stuff that made you feel you were sampling the latest music.

The Record Market was in the arse-end of Redcliffe Arcade, which meant it was reassuringly Redcliffe where boofheads like me would wander in with a choccy thickshake, a head full of pimples, a Brothers blue-and-white butcher-striped rugby jersey and Banana Chunder Stubbies.

The staff used to try to look like they didn't live in Redcliffe, meaning they dressed in black t-shirts with Frank Zappa, The Stranglers or The Ramones printed on the front.

On the particular summer arvo I remember it was a large woman in a Stranglers black t-shirt who was behind the counter.

If we weren't exactly on nodding terms, she certainly knew me as a regular moocher to the store.

David Bowie was warbling away over the store's sound system and, as I sucked away on my thickshake, I turned to the woman and shared my opinion of his classic 'Changes'.

'What a great song,' I mumbled.

The too-cool-for-school shop assistant in her black t-shirt looked over. I tried to sound like I was at footy training talking about a dropkick for goal.

'Good song, this. Not bad.' And I sucked again.

She looked a little surprised that someone dressed like me could appreciate the Thin White Duke's work. And who could blame her? But then who really knows what the next person may be thinking when listening to David Bowie?

She went to say something and thought better of it. But when I said, 'Good old Starman, eh?' as if David Bowie had just dobbed a field goal from outside the quarter line in the corner, she couldn't contain herself and blurted out, 'You look like you've got a wall of Lego bricks in your pants. Or is that where you keep your wallet?'

Then she blushed a bit and looked down at the counter.

I just stood and then broke the silence with a long draining suck on my thickshake.

As I walked back down the arcade, I turned to look at my reflection in the glass windows on the walls. Over yet another suck of the choccy thickshake I pondered, almost Hamlet-like, 'A wall of Lego or my wallet?' It had a 'to be or not to be' ring to it.

It was quite apt that the largish woman had been wearing a Stranglers t-shirt as that was also the effect of the Stubbies non-crotch.

The final nail in the banana boardies came by way of the Smart brothers, Brian and Kevin. They ironically carried the surname of the characteristic of which they were completely devoid – smart.

They weren't stupid, but they were fairly gormless droobs.

Brian, for some reason, insisted he could speak German when it was patently obvious he couldn't. What he emitted from his mouth was a combination of *Commando* war comic phrases and German baddies war movie banter, all strung together at a livestock auctioneers' pace.

When he was asking for a ticket to Sandgate Station it sounded like the bloke from *Von Ryan's Express* asking for a machine gun to shoot Frank Sinatra as he tried to get on the train at the end of the movie. It was all *jawohl, danke, Kommandant, Donner und Blitzen* and *schweinehund* and Sandgate *bitte.*

Once, after Brian had gone through what seemed like half a phone book of gibberish, the bus driver said, 'Where do you want to bloody go, Champ? In English.'

Brian sighed and said, 'Sandgate Railway Station.' Then, as he sat down after being given his ticket, he sighed again, loudly. 'Can I help it if Australia isn't a bilingual country?'

The bus driver muttered back. 'Maybe try Austria instead.'

The other odd thing about Brian was he always behaved like he was in a cowboy movie, trying to walk like John Wayne, easing himself through doorways as if he expected he'd have to draw a non-existent gun at any moment.

He'd sit with his back to the wall in class or at the Piccadilly Café opposite the Redcliffe Jetty as if he was Alan Ladd from *Shane.* When he got a plastic rain poncho from Kmart, he would wear that, a straw sunhat with green under the brim and strut round with a Winfield Blue ciggy clenched in his teeth like Clint Eastwood. All the time talking in doggerel German.

I think he was just buggerising about, but he took it to a different level.

His brother Kevin, who was older and quite skilled in draftsmanship, was always drawing on himself or his brother in permanent marker; temporary tattoos if you like, which were quite ornate but quite unwittingly esoteric. And also must have been agony to remove, although Kevin always carried a tube of Ipana White toothpaste because he said it would remove any drawing he didn't like.

There was a lack of planning in Kevin's efforts, as evidenced by his writing LOVE on the fingers of one hand and HATE on the other, like Robert Mitchum's character in *The Night of the Hunter*, where he played a homicidal preacher. Kevin was right-handed and had written LOVE on the fingers of his left hand with an immaculate copperplate font, but the effect was diminished somewhat when he had to go with his non-preferred hand for HATE. The result was a rather primitive-looking collection of letters. So you went from the elegant Renaissance on the left to barely junior-level Neanderthal on the right. He said he kind of liked the effect though – LOVE being elegant and HATE being brutal – which wasn't a bad point to make. But the real problem was that he had drawn the letters on with his hands facing himself, so when he thrust out his balled fists to display his handiwork, it had to be pointed out to him that the words were upside down.

Kevin balling his fists then pushing them up to his face as if he was about to strike himself to see the upside-down word, then stretching out his hands flat in front to see the correct word was slightly unnerving.

He did it quickly at first but with each repeated effort his action eventually became almost slow motion, as if he was engaging in some strange martial arts exercise. I actually think he was having trouble comprehending what he had done and when at last it dawned, he looked at his balled fists and said simply, 'Oh, bullshit.'

'*Ja*,' said Brian.

One Saturday Kevin appeared with a beautifully rendered lawnmower on his upper thigh with 'VICTA–Ree' emblazoned above it.

When he was asked what it meant, he said he had misspelt VICTORY and instead of having an Australian flag underneath he had decided to go with the flow and improvised a Victa lawnmower on full attack.

Of course, it was also upside down.

So, that was the Smart brothers, and the end for the Banana Chunder Boardies came when I bumped into them after a rather half-arsed arvo of surfing on the Bribie Island surf beach. I was lying flat out on the beach soaking up a bit of sun and having a break from falling off my board into the waves.

I opened my eyes when my name was called by Brian Smart. He was standing above me and was fully dressed in double denim with a huge plastic cowboy hat on his head.

'You look like you've got a rudimentary sundial for your dick, Willy.'

'Yeah?' I said, and motioned to my tortured Stubbies crotch. 'Well, I guess it's time you pissed off.'

He half laughed and walked back off the beach.

The last straw came after I made my way up and saw both brothers standing in the carpark.

I couldn't quite believe what they were wearing. Kevin was in a pair of disco board shorts covered in shining sequins and Brian, again in his purple plastic cowboy hat, appeared from behind a toilet like a Western hero making sure the coast was clear until he presented himself in a pair of white swimmers with a belt and little pictures of the *Hindenburg* printed all over them.

We nodded to each other and then, for no accountable reason, in a rather bland, almost disinterested tone, Kevin pointed to the Stubbies board shorts I wore and said, 'Those boardies just scream loser. You look like such a deadshit in them, Willy.'

Brian chimed in, '*Ja*, so *ist es* . . . deadshit.'

I shrugged my shoulders. I walked on. I stuck the old Malibu on top of the car, strapped it down and drove back towards home. About twenty minutes later there was a turn into one of the servos that dotted the Bruce Highway, not far from the weighbridge and the place that sold houses on stumps.

I got out, took my cricket whites and went into the servo toilets.

After being bagged by the Smart brothers, I finally took the hint. I binned the Stubbies for good. I put on my whites, got back in the car and drove home.

•

After the Banana board shorts I lived in the world of rather anonymous swimwear, sticking firm with Ruggers and the odd Golden Breed boardies. It was the Smugglers that lured me back.

Budgie Smugglers.

An English friend, quite appropriate really considering an English corporation had swallowed up Speedo, asked me once why 'Speedo swimming briefs' (her words) were called Budgie Smugglers.

'Well, why do you think?' I asked, expecting the matter to be straightforward.

She gave me a rather deadpan look. 'I don't know – that's why I'm asking.'

I asked her if she was familiar with budgies.

'The small parrots? Budgerigars? Yes, my mother keeps them.'

I loved the British accent saying something as innocuous as, 'Yes, my mother keeps them' because it sounded slightly rapacious. There was something 'Joseph Banksian' about the collection of a native species; the treasures of empire being 'kept'.

'Good for her,' I said of my friend's mother's budgies/ treasures of empire. I went on. 'Now, imagine a budgie – a small parrot – being smuggled in a wrapping of nylon, Spandex and Lycra.'

She frowned slightly and nodded. Then, as if she were a detective inspector in some English police drama on the ABC on a Sunday night following the mounting evidence in a crime, said, 'Go on.'

'Well now, the next time you see a bloke wearing Speedo swimming briefs, try thinking of his tackle as a small parrot. Which is being smuggled.'

The police inspector frowned in thought and then the mental pictures and their meaning crept across her face.

'Oh! Oh God!' She laughed. 'Oh yes! His cock and balls are the smuggled budgerigar! That's marvellous.'

I accepted her appreciation of Australian slang but had to point out that Cock and Balls and the Smuggled Budgerigar sounded like two English Pubs – perhaps favourite haunts of the inspector from the police show.

But another thought had come upon her. 'Oh Christ!' she gasped and put her hands to her face and closed her eyes for a moment. Then she laughed again and said, 'My mother has this party trick where she will take her budgerigars out of the cage and hold them on her fingers – I cannot now unsee the contents of swimming briefs perched on Mum's index finger and her mumbling sweet pleasantries to it!'

She was a good egg, the police inspector, and took to Australian English heartily. About a month after I had explained Budgie Smugglers to her we sat with other pals over a beer in a hotel in Bondi.

A bearded bloke walked past our table and there were a few mumbles and laughter.

I asked why.

Another friend explained that the police inspector and she had been swimming laps at the city baths and had seen this bearded bloke exiting from the pool. The police inspector had said to our mutual pal after the beard walked past them, 'Oh lord, forget budgies, he's an albatross smuggler.'

The Budgie Smuggler was fine for purpose swimming – like lap swimming or occasionally open sea swimming – but it was a bit much for a recreational lounge on the beach or a friendly float in the water.

And sometimes, worn out of the context of these more athletic summer pursuits, the wearing of these garments can lead to a case of Budgie Smuggler-cide. The wearer is often totally ignorant about how the garment can affect those close to them. But still, for some reason, I kept coming back to the Smugglers.

They were easy to pack and quick to dry, so what was not to like? They became a bit of a habit.

In my early middle age my family and I had gone to the beach for a week around New Year and I had conveniently forgotten my sensible middle-aged boardies and had instead encased myself in a rather generous pair of navy-blue Smugglers that were the final word in comfort.

I had bought them on sale, where they had been the only item left hanging forlorn on the rack. Like the runt of a litter of pups, but just as that runt turns out to be a true and steadfast hound, these Smugglers were loyal and never let me down. It was love at first wear.

How long can a relationship last with a piece of clothing? Well, longer than someone's prime ministership in Australia. I can say quite confidently that those Smugglers saw John Howard in and out.

But perhaps the holiday was a Budgie Smuggler too far because even the noblest servant can spread themselves too thin. Literally.

I can't say I wasn't warned or given hints. On an earlier holiday we had gone to the Gold Coat and had ended up at one of the many 'worlds' that tourist mecca has to offer. My Smugglers and I were just about to embark on the delights of Wet 'n' Wild, a theme park full of pools, slides, plunges and shrieking humanity, when my wife pointed a finger at me and said levelly, 'You are not going on these slides wearing THOSE THINGS.'

When I stared blankly at her she added, 'There are children here.'

I sort of understood what that meant and I made a dash to the theme park's shop where I found a collection of slightly porky, blank-gazed men about my age huddled around a stand selling more appropriate garb. Baggy black shorts. 'One size fits all!' said one of our band breathlessly.

Suitably attired, I was ready to make a big splash. And it was not the first time I appreciated the astonishing power and simple joy of being a human in water. For a place that is so attuned to being body-conscious, the Gold Coast's theme park was an oasis of acceptance and commonality. All shapes and sizes heaved and ran and shot around the complex, swept along by the elemental joy of water.

On a birthday before our New Year holiday, my wife had bought me a pair of extra-long Canterbury rugby training shorts that she said were just right for the beach. These were the boardies I had forgotten to pack.

One morning on the beach in the first week of the New Year, my wife put down the book she had been reading while I got the kids out of the water, the youngest hugging my leg as we dragged ourselves across the sand. My wife asked why I insisted on wearing those 'THINGS'. I told her I had forgotten my birthday boardies. She said that was a handy coincidence.

I realised she thought I had planned to wear the Smugglers. I told her they were smashingly comfy.

She asked why I always spoke like I was from a generation about forty years in the past. You must remember that she was once asked to describe me and uttered this unique summation: 'William was born wearing a cardigan and humming a Perry Como tune.'

'What's wrong with "comfy"?' I asked, genuinely perplexed.

'Those THINGS make you look like one of those old plonkers from World Championship Wrestling.'

As soon as she saw my reaction, she knew she had made a mistake.

World Championship Wrestling was a golden moment from a generation's childhood, it was on telly on a Sunday morning, screening after Mass, along with the Speedway results and *Sportscene*.

It mustn't be confused with the super-hyped, steroid-enhanced rubbish of WWE, World Wrestling Entertainment, home of clowns like Hulk Hogan and The Undertaker.

To each their own, but World Championship Wrestling from the days of black-and-white TV was filled with blokes that could have been friends of your father, or if not friends then they would certainly have been customers of his hire business.

Mario Milano perhaps would hire trestles, Bulldog Brower a cement mixer and because Larry O'Dea, the Laughing Irishman, was a flog, he'd probably just hire a plank and not know what to do with it.

Comparing World Championship Wrestling to WWE is like comparing Dwight D. Eisenhower to Donald Trump – there really is no point because the former is light years better than the latter. Even those who recognised the pantomime of World Championship Wrestling couldn't help but like it – people like my father who thought 'the whole show was just bad play acting' and yet when he caught a bout where Mario Milano was going through one of his turns and grabbing any living thing he could get his hands on and throwing it as far as he could, my Old Man delightfully howled the legendary line. 'Jesus, Mary and Joseph, that big Eyetie is a mighty grappler!'

World Championship Wrestling was such wonderful daggy fun and the moves were so telegraphed and hopeless that they were easily mimicked and performed.

Especially down at the beach or the local pool, where you could pretend to propel yourself off the turnbuckle and flop into the water. Or you could take a deep breath and then somersault over one of your sisters or a mate underwater.

Even my Old Man would sometimes join in, rising from the water and leaping out at you, swinging wildly, all the while adding a commentator's voice: 'Here comes Captain Canada but his blows have no effect upon Captain Australia!'

You would pretend to push him away and he would fling himself into the water with a great splash and then he would emerge again, this time as another opponent – always members of the Commonwealth and always with the rank of Captain – 'Now it's Captain Kenya's turn!'

You'd push him away again and he'd cry loudly before going under the water crying out guff like, 'Oh! No luck there for the plucky African! But good on ya, Kenya!'

It was wonderful, silly, lovely fun.

And all done in baggy, smashingly comfortable swimming trunks. If only my dad could wear proper wrestling attire – he was big and strong and loud. He'd be a smash on World Championship Wrestling. Killer Colin Mac!! If only he'd wear the right wrestling daks.

Close to one Father's Day, my mother and I were walking along Redcliffe Parade past Kelly Sports Store where new season swimwear – Budgie Smugglers – was displayed next to a poster of Mario Milano for an upcoming bout of World Championship Wrestling at Festival Hall in Brisbane.

In between the display and the poster, someone had written on a bit of paper, 'AS WORN BY MARIO MILANO!' with an arrow pointing towards the Smugglers. I told my mother we should buy a pair of Mario's for Dad.

She said to me, 'I think your father is quite happy in his trunks, thank you very much.'

I thought all of this while standing before my wife in my Smugglers after she had claimed I looked like those World Championship Wrestling plonkers.

My wife's face fell when she saw my reaction.

I beamed. 'Really?'

For the next ten minutes I cried out names of the plonkers. 'Mario Milano? Spiros Arion? Abdullah the Butcher? Killer Karl Kox? Brute Bernard?'

And I would strike a suitable pose for each of the old wrestlers.

There was a ritual: tugging at the waist of my Smugglers, then clapping loudly with my hands and then splaying my legs and raising my hands in different positions. Our kids joined in, and we went through as many of the old wrestling plonkers as I could remember, there before my wife who sat on the beach, the book she was reading before she mentioned the wrestlers folded in her lap as she laughed occasionally at what we were performing before her.

'Oh,' she said, 'I liked him, do him again.'

I gave her my best Mark Lewin and grabbed my son in the famous 'Maniac' sleeper hold. He struggled like a loon, giggling.

Even Ron Miller, an otherwise anonymous enough old grappler, was asked to pose again as my wife got her ever-present camera from her beach bag and took some snaps.

That night over a wine she downloaded the images she had captured during the day onto her laptop and gave me a wave of her hand to look.

'Here, see what Ron Miller looks like with light behind him on the beach,' was all she said.

I had a squiz. If I had been Kevin Smart I would have said 'Bullshit' slowly, for the image of Ron Miller, me in my aged and gamey Budgie Smugglers, looked as though I was a prime candidate for being Annette Kellerman-ed, that is, arrested.

'Oh dear,' was all I could say.

'Yes,' said my wife.

'Might be time to bin the old Smugglers, I think.' The way I said it sounded like I was going to lead my old roan horse up to the top paddock to be done away with.

My wife laughed a bit and so did I. Then she nodded, put her arms around me and said, 'But I did like Ron Miller.' And she pulled me in for a kiss.

The age of the Smuggler had finally passed.

8

SOUNDS OF SUMMER

Janice from Balmain was saying that one of the sounds of summer for her had to be a kookaburra calling out. 'Oh, Janice, yes, the kookaburra, how much more Australian can we get?' said the rather breathless but well-spoken radio announcer.

It was the ABC, of course, and not for the first time I thought to myself that many in the national broadcaster came from the subspecies of *Homo sapiens* that had been house captains or prefects or class captains or library monitors.

I, of course, had been none of these things and I really should let go of any residual bitterness of not achieving these ranks of honour and privilege during my education.

Before the enthusiastically well-spoken former library monitor was asking people for their summer sounds she had been breathlessly agreeing with a life coach who was of the opinion that people who said they didn't care about achieving anything at primary or high school were engaging in an 'understandable self-defensive strategy' of not seeking advancement – 'they ambush their ambition'.

I really should have stopped listening then, but I was on a jag. I hadn't slept very well; I was away from home for work, and it was three quarters of the way through summer.

I was in Sydney staying at an apartment complex that was very comfortable, with very helpful staff, although the long hallways were like a cross between a sideshow alley maze of mirrors and a scene from the Stanley Kubrick film *The Shining*. I kept expecting to see two dark-haired twins holding hands and smiling their creepy smiles whenever I got lost trying to find my room, but at least there were no gushing hallways of blood or room service folk trying to come in through the door with an axe yelling, 'Here's Johnny!' à la Jack Nicholson, so I was thankful for that.

The other thing that struck me about the apartment was how its name sounded like 'edema', the condition where fluid builds up in the tissues of your body, usually in the legs and around the ankles.

This was slightly unfortunate as the apartment was, as I have stated, comfortable and full of friendly and helpful staff, but I couldn't stop myself from calling the place The Edema.

So I am in Sydney, three quarters of the way through summer and on a jag, listening to the radio, which is irritating me.

I should have turned it off, but I couldn't quite muster the effort and, to be honest, it was hit or miss if I could turn it off. The thing was tuned through the TV, which had a habit of turning itself back on after I tried to switch it off. That may sound like a scene from the Japanese horror classic *Ringu*, but it was more to do with the fact that there were two remotes in the room and I had lost one.

It was somewhere among the detritus on the floor, or perhaps even in the bed and when I inadvertently touched it the TV/radio would come on or off at inopportune moments.

So I had given up on terminating the sound and let matters take their own course. That's how I found myself sitting on the end of the bed, with the air conditioning turned down as far as it would go – 19 degrees – and a fan on a pedestal that lurched at an ungainly angle turned up as fast as it could turn – setting 4.

The fan had been kindly brought to me by a staff member who I think came from Bangladesh, after another front desk staff member, who came from Brazil, had tried to turn the air conditioner down but was told by a staff member from housekeeping, who came from Senegal, that the air conditioning was centrally controlled and couldn't drop further than 19 degrees.

Sydney's summer was so swelteringly humid I could do no more than sit, listen and talk to Janice about the kookaburras in Balmain.

'Is that just a sound of summer, Janice? Kookaburras call in all seasons!' I pronounced.

Is there anything more pathetic than a cranky, middle-aged moaner draped in the cloak of a humid Sydney summer talking back to a radio he doesn't know how to turn off?

Yes, there is.

I suddenly realised that my voice sounded astoundingly like Robert Kennedy Jnr's – the rather odd United States Health Secretary under Donald Trump and Robert Kennedy's son. That's what happens when you talk through a lurching fan on full throttle.

I stopped and then said, 'I like falconry and eating road kill,' which were both hobbies and passions of the American Health Secretary. I kind of liked the way falconry sounded as if I was swearing, so I said it over and over for a while. And then laughed.

There is a sound of Sydney summer for you, Janice: air conditioning, that constant unsatisfying soft drone, and a leaning fan blazing at full throttle in your face, making you look like a dog with a drooling tongue hanging out of a speeding car's window. In a moment of fancy I imagined I was like Captain Bill Taylor who, in 1935, was crossing the

Tasman Sea in the crippled *Southern Cross* piloted by Charles Kingsford Smith. Not familiar with Bill? What a bloke – he was the fellow who got out on a wing and took the oil from one engine and put it in the tank of the engine on the other wing just so the plane could make it back to Sydney.

And all the while I am sounding like the very strange, raspy, wavery-voiced disgraced scion of an American political dynasty.

It might have been the humidity, but I also wondered if anybody else at that exact moment in Sydney was thinking of RFK Jnr, Smithy and the *Southern Cross*. And Bill Taylor too, of course. I said through the fan very slowly, 'Captain Bill Taylor.'

The Sounds of Summer indeed.

'I know they call all through the year,' Janice was saying, 'but I just heard one this morning and it struck me as being the perfect summer sound.'

'Well, I can't argue with that, can I?' I RFK Jnr-ed through the fan.

'Oh, Janice,' said the breathless library monitor, 'if that is what summers mean to you, then that's summer.'

I supposed the breathless library monitor had a point.

Another caller called Fran said she loved the sound of a water sprinkler because it made her think of children playing. I just sat and thought, yes, okay, Fran, you may have something there.

And as I thought that, the breathless library monitor said, 'Oh Fran, I think you may have something there, I think we can all fill in the dots.'

I know it was the humidity but was the breathless monitor inside my head? Was I in hers? 'Rubbish!' I Robert Kennedy Junior-ed again. And just to be safe I said, 'There's no room for you in there, the worm takes up most of it.'

Then Fran asked if she could be greedy and share another sound.

'If you're quick,' said the breathless library monitor and Fran said yes, she would be quick and she managed to get out, 'Cicadas', how she used to love the sound as a kid and how you knew it was summer when the cicadas made that racket. Then poor old Fran got cut off, maybe she was too greedy or someone pushed the wrong button in the studio. The breathless library monitor almost eulogised Fran. 'Oh, we've lost her. We've lost Fran. But what a wonderfully evocative sound she gave us; I can almost hear the squeals of delight when that sprinkler starts, and as for cicadas — or is it cicatas? You say cicada, I say cicata — they certainly do make a racket.'

I decided I had gone off the breathless library monitor, but she was probably just trying to fill airtime while the operator worked out where all the callers had gone. 'Oh, poor Fran,' she said wanly.

'Christ,' I said into the fan, 'Fran isn't dead, she just lost the connection.'

•

Are they clichéd sounds? Kookaburras calling out? Sprinklers? Cicadas – it definitely is cicada, library monitor – singing?

I mean those sounds could be combined for a McDonald's ad flogging some concocted vision of Australia to sell some dodgy drive-through food.

But even clichés are based in some sort of truth we've all experienced, or think we've experienced.

Once you associate a sound with summer, it's locked away somewhere in the kitbag between your ears and can pop out at any time or just lie around in the litter with all the memories. Just like the TV remote covered by clothes, papers and whatever else lay on the floor in that hotel room.

Take me: I would forever associate the Edema with summer. Just because of the wretched stillness and the smothering humidity. I was told by an Argentinian person who worked alongside the Brazilian on the front desk that the humidity was caused by climate change, that the waters of the coast were warming.

I asked him how long he'd been in Australia, and he told me eight months. I didn't say anything, but he added, 'Sir, the science is everywhere. I can read and I also have a degree in marine biology.'

Maybe he thought I might complain that he'd said something that somebody on the front desk shouldn't be saying, but I certainly didn't want anybody to get in trouble for saying what they thought.

I nodded. He was probably right, or it might just be the way Sydney is these days, either way all I wanted was for the change to come. The cool change and rain that was promised almost hourly by the least respected soothsayer in history – the BOM, the Bureau of Meteorology. In any event the best I could offer was, 'It is certainly hot and sticky.'

'Indeed,' he said.

I could associate all the accents that I heard in this part of Sydney with being sounds of summer. Even that night I couldn't sleep, as well as the *Southern Cross*'s fan roaring away, I was kept awake by a deep rumbling from the next little balcony along to mine.

I got up, and, not unlike Captain Bill Taylor wing-walking over the Tasman Sea, I gingerly made my way through the darkened room and the sliding doors to the outside. I felt the slab of humid air hit me and listened.

I inched along the small verandah.

The rumbling was a voice; the deep bass voice of the occupant of the room next door. He was on his verandah having a phone conversation which all seemed one way from his end. He sounded like the entire bass section of the Red Army Choir phoning in the chorus from the 'Song of the Volga Boatmen', which didn't make for pleasant late-night listening.

It was like the sound of some villain from a *Taken* movie Liam Neeson might make, and even though I didn't have dear old Liam's particular set of skills and wasn't going to find the villain and kill him, I summoned up the Neeson within and offered up words that were more token than *Taken*.

'Come on, Champ, it's two-thirty in the morning. Rein it in, will you?'

There was a pause and then, à la *Taken*, I received, in a thick Russian accent the short reply, 'Sorry, Cobber, I will go inside. I cannot sleep.'

'You're not the only one; too warm.'

'Climate change.'

Who would have thought that a *Taken* villain would be on the 'right' side of the climate culture wars?

And the Red Army Bass Chorus went inside.

•

The area where I was staying was described to me by a work colleague as being 'Hyper Bondi', a collection of cafés, eateries, bars and gyms that teamed with people who all looked very much the same but sounded different.

One morning, I was heading out to grab a coffee and I heard a couple in front of me talking about the place we'd all found ourselves in. They were probably about ten years older than me, and they were walking through the Edema's lobby as if they were leaving the saloon in a western movie to step out onto the street for a gunfight.

There was something oddly fatalistic about their tone, a little like Kevin Costner and Robert Duvall in *Open Range*. Again, I suppose it was the humidity at work.

'Just think, I wanted to go to Europe this year,' said the woman without much humour.

'If the idea was to bump into Europeans, you don't need to bother because they all seem to be over here, and half of South America too.'

'Well, the younger set, perhaps,' and they both laughed.

'The Younger Set', such a funny term. They both must have been a part of the 'Younger Set' many years ago.

The Younger Set of Hall Street were another sub-species and some of the sounds of summer they emitted will long haunt my memory.

So many accents. As soon as you spoke to the front desk or hit the street, the braying of the English in bars, the singsong of the Irish and Scots, the definite-ness of the Americans, the clipped Kiwis and machine-gun rapidity of countless other voices speaking in their own languages, all there in Hyper Bondi. A wall of human sound, a concerto of humans being humans.

The tribe of Hall Street were indeed another sub-species, perhaps Backpacker-us Obnoxious or Hall-us Erectus Fitus or perhaps Airheadus Humongous. I don't know but they certainly seemed to be a different stream of the human experiment and to say that I stood out like dog's balls in their company is an understatement.

First, they were all dressed as if they were going to a party where the theme was athletic wear, and the idea was to wear as little of the athletic wear as possible and not be arrested.

They were very fit, very tanned and very made-up. And if they weren't in a couple or with friends, they all seemed to have earbuds connecting them to their phones and to whoever was on the other end of the digital device. And even if they were in a couple or with friends, chances were they had earbuds anyway, which meant that they all spoke with great intensity and great energy at the same time to someone who wasn't with them. So, along with the noise of all the accents from in-person conversations, an extra layer of disconnected chatter was added, lending to the cacophonous noise of human sound. A sound of summer.

They almost looked like a crowd of AI-generated images of what people might look like in an imagined world where you had nothing to do but parade around.

What interested me most was the tan at play on the streets of Bondi. Bronzing would have been a more accurate term, for that terracotta finish covering limbs and body that appeared in between the suggestion of athletic apparel had nothing to do with the sun above.

Probably done at a salon, or maybe we've all moved past that. There must have been some product you could use to give yourself a quick cut and polish at home in your preferred room or maybe a tablet that could change you from inside to out.

Not for the first time, I remembered the words of an old pal when confronted with what he described as an epidemic of fake tan-itis. We'd been having dinner when a horde of young people dressed to the nines but with skin tones ranging from gold to mandarin to brown and deep mahogany all noisily jostled past. My pal took them in, had a sip of his wine and said, 'Isn't it ironic how our nation, which had once been so violently in favour of upholding the White Australia Policy, has journeyed to the point where the descendants of that policy's proponents adorn themselves with the camouflage of skin colours that would have them deported in the "good old days" .'

He raised his glass. 'Here's to progress.'

Suntans.

I remembered the old television advertisement from the anti-cancer 'Slip, Slop, Slap' a singsong campaign designed to make Australians aware of the dangers of skin cancer if you didn't cover up with clothes or sunscreen. In hindsight, our failure to do so seems the height of madness.

A bit of zinc on the lips and nose and Bob's your uncle, away you go, bare-chested. If you wore a hat it was a ridiculous tiny terry-towelling creation plonked upon your head like a badly constructed pavlova that wouldn't give any protection at all.

So many of those cricketing heroes – Richie Benaud with his shirt unbuttoned down to his ankles as my mother said, Ian Chappell and so many others – had issues with skin damage that came to haunt them in later years. Even humble boofheads like me would have to make treks to our dermatologist to have bits and pieces sliced from different parts of our bodies like a Christmas ham.

Even worse was the way people would not slip, slop and slap on protective sunscreen but instead lather themselves in suntan oils to get that longed-for tan.

At the Redcliffe War Memorial pool in Sydney Street the lawn would be covered with people, mostly women, stretched out like kebabs, glistening in the sun. And we stupid boys, in our early to mid-teens, would pretend to go to the toilet up there in the corner by the Anne Shearer Kindy just so we could clumsily wade through the frying kebabs, copping an eyeful.

I remember one of the kebabs raised herself up a bit and said to me after we had repeated the exercise a number of times, 'Rack off, dickhead. Go and cop a perv somewhere else.'

Half embarrassed and half excited that one of the frying kebabs – an actual young woman – had spoken to me, I ran off, slipped on the cement walkway and awkwardly plunged into the pool while, over the PA system, came the perennial summer sound of, 'No bombing in the pool, no bombing.'

Keep your kookaburras, Janice, I'll take 'Rack off, dickhead. Go and cop a perv somewhere else . . . no bombing in the pool, no bombing!'

I suddenly remembered a boy at Humpybong who had been out playing cricket on the weekend and whose nose had been burnt bright red entertaining us at little lunch by peeling some of his sunburnt skin off and trying to get the longest bits with one careful delicate drag of his fingers.

The boy with the burnt nose would say, 'Listen, listen, you can hear it come off, my skin. Listen to my skin.'

And some of us would dip our heads towards him as he pulled at his burnt skin. When it was my turn, I strained to listen but heard nothing until another boy standing close let out a huge fart and we all laughed.

Another said, 'Your skin stinks as bad as it sounds.'

And the boy with the sunburnt nose repeated, 'I can hear my skin!'

But nobody was really interested anymore. I suppose a good fart can steal anybody's thunder.

All these years later, I can still hum the tune of the 'Slip, Slop, Slap' commercial in my head. After a while, it became a part of the way Australians spoke about summer.

I walked amongst the Younger Set and hummed and then softly sang the lyrics, 'Slip on some sunscreen and slap on a hat.'

And I had one of those memories, one of those sounds of summer which leap up from the detritus of the kitbag between the ears and hit your heart square on.

It was a memory of a girl, a lovely woman I had known in the final year of uni. She was the person who had encouraged me to audition for WAAPA as well as enrol in law.

'Just to see how it goes; if you like it. You can say you tried, better than never knowing.' And she smiled.

I thought her lovely because I never really knew that I wanted to even try.

We were at a beach one afternoon back in the day and she had held my hand and pulled me back from walking to the water. She had pulled me close and said, 'Come on, you, slip, slop, slap!'

She offered me her sunscreen and then poured a bit in her hands and put it on my face. Not slapping or slopping but gently and she sang the song as she did it. To finish off, she tapped my nose and kissed me on my sun-screened lips and then ran off laughing into the water.

Chuck in seagulls' cries, which she loved, and the sound of the beach and there, Janice, is a summer sound enough for any man.

And then I felt that sad pang when you suddenly remember a life that shared your life for a time. Almost as if you were both punctuation marks in the other life. What would that punctuation mark be? A comma – a pause in the journey;

an exclamation mark – meaning strong feelings like sorry, anger or joy; or a full stop, meaning finality.

Or perhaps the ellipsis, those three dots which mean there's no need for words, but perhaps there's a pause and a suggestion there's something left unsaid.

But there's nothing really to be said except to wonder what happened to her and how she got on. Well, I hoped.

Perhaps I wasn't singing as softly as I thought because a very chiselled and manscaped face had looked up at me. Not a blemish of any sun damage on his handsome mug.

'Sorry,' I said.

'Hey.' He smiled a perfect smile, 'Don't say sorry, it's cute. Singing a song from . . . the old days?'

He paused before he said 'old days' like he didn't want to give offence. 'Good energy,' he said and then turned back to the front and stood like a model from a glossy magazine like the rest of his tribe.

•

I looked at the couple standing in front of me in the line to order coffee. Although I wouldn't really call what they were doing standing. Posing would be more apt – carefully standing just so to display the body of work they had spent so much time on to the best advantage.

Others were doing it too: checking the form and shape of others of their species. One woman at the front of the café was almost prone in a sun-lounger, which you'd usually see around a pool instead of a café, but it gave her the chance to be half reclined as if she was in the middle of doing a sit-up. Her abdomen was flexed for greatest effect while she ate slices of avocado and an omelette made from egg white.

When the couple in front of me entered the café, she looked them up and down and her eyes did something odd, like a jungle cat sizing up another animal of their species – not directly looking at them but seeing them, almost sensing them.

It was like a nature wildlife documentary.

It would be wrong to say it was overtly sexual but it was certainly a way of gauging where one creature stood in terms of another.

As for me, I was deemed of no interest at all, save for the oddity of being some old coot who was humming tunes from the old days.

I was just something to be navigated, like a hole in the footpath or a large structure inconveniently placed in the path. I blended into the basic terrain. And in an odd way, even though I was more of a burly Gerald Durrell than a David Attenborough, I was being given a bird's-eye view of how this group of exotic beings interacted.

And just to top off accents as a sound of summer, the exchange I heard in front of me was something that, had I not witnessed and overheard it, I would have put down to a collection of tall tales on some website or social media post.

The sound that came from the young couple could perhaps be described as Hall Street English. It was half cooing and oo's, ahh's, and uhhhha's, as if the King's Singers were trying to start up some odd chorus.

The couple wanted coffees: a long black with a block of ice and an almond milk latte, decaf.

Almond milk. Unless nuts had been grown with teats, from which milk could be extracted, then what they wanted in the coffee wasn't any form of milk.

Teats on nuts. I will leave it there.

The woman held up an energy bar and proceeded to leave the King's Singers in the dust as far as odd sounds were concerned.

'Ahh, could you-uha tell if this uhhha,' she held up an energy bar, 'uh is this-uh GMO free uh?'

The woman behind the counter took the energy bar and said, 'GMO?'

'Uhha GMahhhOO free uh.'

The woman behind the counter said the label should tell if there were any genetically modified organisms in the energy bar.

'Ooouha,' said the woman in the flowerpot tan and athletic apparel, 'living uh organisms? Why would they do that?'

'What?' said the woman behind the counter.

'Put uh living organs . . . in . . . organisms in food?'

'Sorry?' said the woman behind the counter.

She was lost and so was I.

'Uhuh, you know. Why put them in there, like they do in the Chinese?'

There was a silence and the male in athletic apparel said, 'In Chinese uh food.'

I stifled a laugh and the look on the face of the woman behind the counter was priceless.

'MSG?'

'I don't wany-uh the bar company messaging me – can't you tell meuh?'

The woman behind the counter took a deep breath and was very polite. She told the apparel-wearers that MSG was monosodium glutamate, which was sometimes added to some meals for taste. GMO was genetically modified organism, where a plant or food, which is a living organism, has its character changed or modified.

'You know, like how a lot of oils and grains can be changed in a laboratory.'

Or like maybe how almond nuts can be modified to have teats, I almost said.

'And,' she finished, 'nobody will be messaging you from the energy bar people.'

The pause was filled with a gracious sound of apology.

'UHa ohh sorry,' said the woman.

'That is completely fine,' said the woman behind the counter. She read the bar's label. 'No GMO marked, and no MSG, this is all natural.'

'Uho, like me,' the woman in the athletic apparel said. And laughed and added, 'Thuhanks.'

She took her bar, and they turned to check their phones and wait for the coffees, but before doing so the young man with the chiselled jaw turned to me and said, 'Keep that singing up, good energy.'

I nodded.

•

Sitting on the bed in my Edema apartment I remembered walking with my coffee and thinking how all the accents sounded like an incessant droning tone. And I thought of bug catchers. And a cicada. Not a cicata.

Almost every child of a certain generation was at some time, at some birthday or Christmas, given a bug catcher. It was supposed to lead to hours of fun and adventure as the children who used it could collect creatures in their backyards or parks and creeks nearby. It was a see-though plastic container with a funnel-cum-handle at the top and on the bottom a cylindrical shaped chamber with a removable floor that could separate to snare insects and perhaps small reptiles like skinks.

It always had the appearance to me of being a small-scale model for a theme park kiosk.

In any case, given the number of things among the creepy crawly brigade in Australia that can kill or at the very least issue a nasty bite, it was a plaything of a rather bygone and adventurous time.

The television ad showed game outdoors kids separating the bottom from the bug catcher and then holding the two pieces in either hand while they stalked their prey. Slowly they would close in and say, 'Ahhhhhh, gotcha!' Then they'd snare the bug and close the two pieces together, and there in the plastic chamber was your prize.

If you were really game, you could leave the daddy-long-legs behind and maybe snare a huntsman spider. How long you kept them was up to you.

On really hot days cicadas were a prized target.

Cicadas contract their muscles, and a ribbed membrane vibrates, making a noise that is amplified when it resonates in the hollow part of their abdomen.

That sound. That cacophonous noise that on really hot days is almost like a dull roar, a soundtrack from a science fiction film. It's part buzzing, part clicking and part whine, both high pitched and low. Cicadas: an insect orchestra of perfect monotone white noise.

Whenever I see the famous Australian Impressionist painting, *Down on His Luck* by Frederick McCubbin, of a lonely swagman contemplating how his life has led him to this point, where he sits without overt emotion, simply staring into the smoke of his rather sparse campfire, I can hear the din of cicadas.

I know they are there in the bush that surrounds him.

That imagined sound imbues the painting with a fatalistic quality that I find disquieting, a little moving and forlorn but very human.

Where I grew up there seemed to be thousands of cicadas and they all had different names that sounded like trotters or racehorses: Double Drummer, Floury Baker, Clanger, Greengrocer and Yellow Monday.

Some kids would catch them and trade them, but I never got to that point and I think it was because of my father.

On one impressively hot Sunday when the cicadas were going gangbusters I was told to get outside by my mother and find something to do. So I grabbed my old bug catcher and mooched through the yards trying to find something to capture. I was in luck and 'Ahhhh Gotcher-ed' a Double Drummer as it was going about its business on the trunk of a tree.

What a strange-looking fantastical thing, no wonder you thought of a soundtrack to a sci-fi film when they made their sound, so amazing did they look.

Inside the bug catcher was a pretend plastic leaf and twig protruding through the perforated floor. The cicada dwarfed them.

It didn't do much, but I'd caught it so I kept it in the catcher and plonked it on the back verandah where I found my father sitting in yet another one of his 'chairs' — these things were distributed around the house and were for his use.

He'd come up on the back verandah in the late afternoons and sit and ruminate so I was going to move on and take my bug catcher and Double Drummer with me. But he looked at me. 'Hey, come here, Cabbagehead, and show us what you've got.'

I offered up my bug catcher and Double Drummer.

The old man looked at the cicada like it was a fine bottle of wine. Then he looked at me.

'What are you going to do with him?' he asked.

I said I didn't know.

My dad made a face.

I told him I might take the cicada to school, for some kids did that, take it for show and tell, maybe.

I wondered how my dad knew the cicada was a he.

'Show and tell, maybe,' he repeated.

I nodded.

'You know why they make such a racket, these things?' he asked.

I shook my head. I knew he was trying to make a point about something.

My father said, 'There's a fella up in Scarborough who I did a bit of work for, on this shed in the backyard. He's a bloke from the uni in Brizzy. Smart bloke. Science. The cicadas were going off just like now,' my dad said, 'and this smart bloke, he tells me about them. He said they're singing when they make that racket. So, to them, to that fella there,' and he pointed to the creature in the bug catcher, 'they're singing a love song to find a . . .' He paused, trying to find the right word for a twelve-year-old. 'A girl cicada.'

It was the 'bloke cicadas' that sang, the girls didn't say much.

My father thought for a moment then went on. 'It's a bit like how I think your brother's music is a racket but maybe when he's playing his records, the Flagship,' that was my father's name for his eldest son, 'is thinking about . . . you know, love songs . . . girls, maybe.'

I nodded.

'Was this one making a racket, was he singing when you caught him?'

I said I thought he was.

'And now he's not?'

I looked at the cicada. 'I guess he's not.'

My father nodded. 'You know, boy, these fellas don't get to live that long, and it seems a bit of a shame to keep him there to just "maybe" take him to show and tell.'

He picked up the bug catcher and looked at the cicada and then back to me. 'So why don't you let him have a crack, eh? Let him get back out there, chance his arm with his love song? Let's see how he goes?'

He gave me the bug catcher. 'Your decision, you caught him.'

All around the cicadas in the garden sang their rackety love song, so I knew what to do. I looked at the cicada, then lifted the lid from the bottom and he flew off.

My Old Man looked at me and I met his eyes. He just nodded and said quietly to me, 'Good man.'

I didn't use the bug catcher again.

But occasionally out and about, even to this day, I'll come across the discarded shell or casing of a moulted cicada and will think to myself, how did you get on with your love song?

•

There are apparently two hundred types of cicadas to be found in Australia, and nearly as many accents on the street below my apartment. Were the Younger Set down there singing a love song to someone? Or were they just droning? Maybe I was droning. I'll take the latter. Indulging in reverse anthropomorphism isn't really a way to treat humans, however oddly they may clothe themselves.

I went back to sitting in front of my fan.

Songs. There is always a song of summer. Some purpose-built song for celebrating the season of bounty and living life to the fullest. You don't have to go far to find them.

'In the Summertime' by Mungo Jerry, 'Summer Love' by Sherbet, 'Here Comes Summer' by Jerry Keller, 'Summer

Nights' from *Grease* sung by two of the oldest-looking high school students known to mankind – Olivia Newton-John and John Travolta, 'Summertime Sadness' by Lana Del Rey, the truly underrated gem from Ol' 55, '(Feels like a) Summer's Night', 'The Boys of Summer' – one of the great self-pitying middle-aged ditties by Don Henley, 'Summer of '81' by Mondo Rock and even George Gershwin's 'Summertime', which has been sung by everyone from Ella Fitzgerald to Janis Joplin to Lana Del Rey.

There are always summer songs, just as there are always Christmas songs, good and bad.

Then there are the songs that for some reason take hold through summer and become synonymous with that time of year, like Cold Chisel's wonderful 'Khe Sanh' or Daddy Cool's 'Eagle Rock'. One or the other is always cranked up somewhere in a pub or some club and you find yourself drunkenly stumbling through the song, mis-singing or losing the lyrics. In the case of 'Khe Sanh' you totally forget what a wonderful song it is and what it is about. And 'Eagle Rock' is a bit like those interminable hymns that go on forever when you only really need to know the chorus or even the phrase 'Doin' the Eagle Rock!' But at the same whenever you hear them you nod your head and yell, 'SONG!'

Seasonal anthemic songs can sit alongside tunes like Vance Joy's 'Riptide'; those songs that have some odd daydream quality that takes you off to some real or imagined summer place. You can drift in and out of your life like it's some sweet John Hughes teen comedy romance.

Then there are songs that are the sounds of summer simply because at some point the tune became a soundtrack for a moment you remember. Like that time on a hot January afternoon when a thunderstorm was looming and a Russian defector, a lawnmower from the Fartin' Bastard brigade, a cane toad sentinel of soft porn, my father and myself all collided during a life lesson.

The summer of 1979–80 was a cracking time for me, the end of a marvellous year of rolling through my life on a crest of adolescent stupidity and glorious gormlessness. Of simply arsing about. What a wonderful phrase that is: 'arsing about', and if there is ever a time to engage in this delightful, heightened form of human endeavour, it's summer.

I had recently been released from my employment, which was always of a temporal nature, from the Coles New World supermarket in Redcliffe. Even though I'd enjoyed myself immensely the world of retail had decided it could navigate the waters ahead without my assistance.

I had, of course, been spending my time at Coles arsing about, changing my name on my nametags, taking forever to go on trolley-recovery missions, and buggerising around in general – for instance, when I packed the shelves with coffee, I took great delight in turning some of the brands like Maxwell House upside down on the shelves.

It was funny though for when I did get given the push it upset me a little.

My Old Man had told me not to worry and that 'You're all right by me.'

Of course my father being my father had decided one morning for no apparent reason that I needed to learn about hard work and so he came up to me on the side verandah where I hung in a hammock and, like some character out of a crime caper movie, spoke to me like we were going to knock off a bank. 'You get your arse into gear, you're coming with me on a job. Get your work clobber on.'

'What does that mean? I asked.

'Oh, Christ's sake, boy, just put some bloody thongs on, we've got to go.'

The whole thing was fraught because I heard my mother say, 'Oh dear, Colin, you're not taking him with you, are you?'

'Too right,' I heard my father say in answer.

As I walked out, my mother looked over the paper she was reading and said, 'Good luck.'

I stopped when I saw what was in the back of my father's truck, sitting there tied up like a prisoner. A mower. And rakes and tarps. And sacks.

'Oh, Dad, no,' I tried to protest.

'Get in,' was all he said.

We were on a landscaping job. Landscaping. Among his other endeavours, such as house building and his hire business, my father also offered a 'landscaping, lawnmowing and garden rubbish removal service'. It was, as an ad in the *Redcliffe Herald* assured potential customers, 'Efficient and professional'. Well, it was certainly something.

Some of the machines my father had in his fleet of mowers were more novelties than working garden tools. One, a rotary mower, was like a sideshow alley novelty ride, you'd turn the rotor handle as quickly as you could then slam it down in the hope of it starting. It would splutter a bit and hiccup, but that was it. It became known as the Fartin' Bastard.

Thankfully the mower on the back was a pull-start contraption that was part Victa and part Rover, perhaps even part washing machine.

The machines drove my father up the wall and he would at times talk and cajole them into starting and then give up and shake them and swear at them.

This always makes me smile because you cannot escape the gene pool. I have a similar relationship with household appliances – with vacuum cleaners, in particular. My son once artfully observed that I treated vacuum cleaners like a Bond villain does his henchmen. Indeed, I have often muttered a rather colourful and invective-laden version of the Bond Villain line, 'You have disappointed me for the last time,' before the vacuum henchman meets the equivalent of being fed to the sharks.

But as far as mower-throwing was concerned, the Old Man was in a class above. My mother once told me that if lawnmower-throwing was an Olympic sport, 'Your father would be a multi-gold medallist; he'd have more medals than Mark Spitz.'

So off we went. My father decided to fill me in on the caper.

'It's a quick job: in, out. We hit the banana trees and pick up a bit of rubbish and we're out.'

'Why did you bring the mower?'

I could have been asking why we brought shotguns on the bank job.

He looked at me as if I was wet behind the ears and said, 'Looks the part, beefs up the quote and looks like we mean business.' Then he turned away and snapped his head back and yelled, 'Christ alive! Are you in your bloody pyjamas?'

'Well, you told me to just put thongs on.'

'Christ, you are an arsepart!' Then he added, 'Mind your bloody gusset,' and I swore he nearly laughed.

He shook his head and adjusted his cap. This peaked cap was one of his collection of 'dynamic' work hats and looked like the one worn by Robert Shaw when he played the character of Quint the shark hunter in *Jaws*. So my father called it his Quint Special.

My father tugged at the peak of his Quint Special when we pulled up to a small chamfer-board lowset house, and he scanned the target.

The garden looked pretty neat and before my father went in to talk to the householder, he glowered at me and muttered, 'Get the gear off the truck.'

I did as I was told. Just as I was settling the mower down, he prowled up and hissed, 'What's the bloody mower for?'

'You told me to get down the gear.'

'Not the bloody mower. Has it even got any bloody petrol? The bastard of a thing might not even start. Gobshite!'

He bent down and undid the cap.

I looked up. A woman was standing on the small verandah, I could hear music. A record playing. I knew it, a compilation called *Full Boar*. It had a pig's head with sunglasses on the cover. I liked it. The woman smiled and said pleasantly, 'Perhaps you could give the lawn a once-over seeing as you've got the mower.'

My father looked daggers at me, then said heartily, 'Of course, no worries.'

He turned back to me. 'There's a few drops in there, might be able to get around if I'm quick and if the bloody thing starts. Right, let's get stuck in.'

My father was an immensely strong man, and he didn't muck around. I tried not to get in the way, for it was obvious he didn't need me along, but I must admit it was a bit of fun, especially as *Full Boar* played out from an open window in the small house. It was a soundtrack of inanity to the devastating damage that my father in his haste to get the job done was inflicting on the banana trees.

To Rupert Holmes' legendary daggy and seamy song asking if his companion likes piña coladas and walking in the rain, he rained down fierce machete blows and, a few trees later, when The Boomtown Rats wailed through 'I Don't Like Mondays', he even quipped, 'Not sure about Mondays, but they don't like banana trees around here.'

Then he tried to start the mower to Janis Ian's 'Fly Too High'.

He pulled the cord so hard and so frenetically that it looked like it might take off. He was like some mad person in a gym on a piece of fitness equipment and when he changed arms and jumped, I laughed.

He looked up, furious, and ran at me. He chased me halfway round the house while I skipped ahead.

He grabbed me and I could see he was giggling. 'You pie-can,' he said, 'you have a go.'

I walked back and pulled the cord. It started. My father yelled in delight, 'You jammy bugger! You're buying the Tatts ticket tonight! Quick, in under there and get that box of crap she wants gone, I'll feather the mower and do a round of the yard before this bastard craps itself.'

He sounded as if he were trying to pilot a crippled plane home in some crappy film, perhaps like Smithy did in the *Southern Cross*. Did that make me Bill Taylor?

I stopped and looked under the house. It was low to the ground. I'd have to crawl.

'Do I have to? There might be toads.'

'Oh, bugger the toads, grab the box for Christ's sake.' And he was off.

I crawled under the house. I could see my father's big chook legs racing around the yard pushing the mower almost as if he was an old-time film sped up to a ridiculous speed. So much for 'feathering', if the mower was the *Southern Cross* and my dad Kingsford Smith, the crate was getting well and truly flogged.

The mower didn't sound too healthy, and I could hear my father trying to cajole it to a safe landing.

What happened next seemed to take an age but probably didn't even last a few minutes.

I crawled closer to the box. I wanted to get out from under the house. I knew this was the sort of environment where toads would loiter, and I hated toads. I got to the box when Mi-Sex started up with what I always had thought was one of the weaker songs on *Full Boar*, but whoever it was who was playing the record thought differently and they cranked up 'Computer Games'.

I reached the box, tipped it slightly at an angle and saw an old, folded *Courier-Mail* newspaper inside. It was dusty but I noticed the box wasn't. Here we go, I thought.

The Russian defector. Porn.

A mint issue of the first *Australian Penthouse* magazine with the centrefold being the Russian defector, Liliana Gasinskaya. She was actually Ukrainian, but this was in the days of the Soviet Union, so she was as Russian as.

A waiter on a Russian cruise ship, she had squeezed through a porthole and, clad only in a red bikini, swam ashore and sought asylum. She was given it and then was heralded as the first centrefold in *Australian Penthouse.*

My mind raced as my father's legs sped around the house even faster, his voice a bit shrill as he said over and over, 'C'mon, C'mon, C'mon.'

The mower wheezed and spluttered; Mi–Sex Computer Gamed away.

If I could grab the box, I could maybe hide the Russian defector somewhere. Maybe there were more magazines there!

I pulled the box closer and tilted it at a better angle. Behind it was the biggest, most malevolent-looking cane toad I have ever seen. It looked like it wasn't ready to give up the Russian defector.

I stared. It puffed itself up. It waddled forward.

I screamed.

It jumped.

I howled and got out in a crazed hyper crawl with the box in tow.

My father roared up as the chorus of 'Computer Games' went into synth and falsetto overdrive. I rolled clear and then leapt up, hit my head on the house, dropped what I was carrying, spilling the box and its contents everywhere and screamed.

My father shouted, 'Snake?'

I screeched, 'Toad!'

I hadn't hit my head that badly, just clipped it, but I had a habit whenever I did hit my head (even when I got hit playing rugby) of clenching my mouth shut and grunting a sort of growl. It seemed to help. Sometimes I would add a vigorous rubbing of my head as I did on this occasion.

My father hissed for me to, 'Rein it in, you're carrying on like a Pension Day Special who's missed his bloody bus,' (meaning I was behaving like a person who, in my mother's words, 'Wasn't quite right'). He was about to say something else as he bent his head down to see what was under the house but instead he roared at the top of his considerable lungs, 'Jesus Christ alive!'

He moved back like an actor on a wire in a kung fu movie, seemingly paddling and propelling himself with his work boots topped with footy socks. He flew through the air and then grabbed a rake in one motion.

The toad hopped into the daylight and met its fate.

'The bastard's as big as a BLOODY PANZER!' my father roared as he frenetically attacked the wretched creature with the rake.

He moved even more maniacally than when he'd been trying to start the mower, all the while dancing in his work boots and sounding like the Three Tenors while he cried, 'Dirty bastard, filthy bloody swine of a thing.'

I groaned and rubbed my head and carried on like a Pension Day Special at the bus stop.

It was over as soon as it began.

The toad was spent and my father's big chest heaved. The mower sputtered to silence. The woman of the house ran out and looked at the sight before her.

The Panzer Tank toad, the large man in a crumpled cap, striped t-shirt and Stubbies brandishing a battle-scarred rake. His large son in what were obviously pyjama bottoms and thongs, rubbing his head and grunting. And the *Penthouse*, *Playboy* and a raft of other magazines along the *Pix/People* line fanning out like a gambler's winning hand on the grass.

She looked at them, and at me. Perhaps she wondered if my distress had been caused by what lay on the ground before us. I stopped grunting. Her eyes darted back down to the Royal Flush before she let out an ear-piercing scream – 'Dale!' – that seemed to go on for a minute.

Above, at the window of the room where the record played, Dale's head appeared, looking down. Red-headed, freckled and a mouth full of braces. 'Oh, my books,' he moaned gormlessly.

And we all stood motionless as Mi-Sex finished 'Computer Games'. Talk about a song of summer.

Sitting on the bed in front of the fan, I laughed like a drain at the memory. When I caught my breath, I heard something outside. Laughter. Kids' laughter.

The patio of the apartment overlooked a scene vastly different to the one which greeted you out front – Hall Street.

The back was suburban Bondi, some old-fashioned flats, some yards of houses, nothing cosmopolitan or hyper, just a familiar landscape of life. And somewhere, kids laughed. In the time it took for me to get to the small awning, another sound of summer and a memory came from the kitbag.

One afternoon when we lived in West Footscray, when the kids were young enough to be still 'kids', my son about nine and our youngest five, I walked with them and our dog Doug around the local footy cum cricket oval, Hansen Reserve.

It was very hot and humid and still that afternoon. Some other families were out walking too. The children dragged their feet and moaned or commented on how hot and sticky the air was. We walked on. Yet those years, when my children were small, were a time of wonder in many ways. Perhaps because you saw the world along with your kids, through their eyes, and to the young magic can be found at any time. Magic seemed to happen in that funny odd suburb often.

Someone once told me that a particular cicada can sound like the clicking of a large water sprinkler, and they were right. On that apartment's little patio, prompted by that laughter, I closed my eyes and remembered the magic of Hansen Reserve when, for no known reason, the ground's water sprinklers leapt up from their little cavities beneath the turf and erupted in sprays of water, the clicking of the sprinklers sounding out a beat.

The sheer delicious shock of being drenched gave way to the delirium of the moment. My children and those of the other families ran screaming, howling with laughter as they were hit with the water then dancing through the jets across the field. Dougie leapt up trying to snap at the water in abandon.

Your clothes were soaked and your lungs empty from laughter.

And as suddenly as it started, it stops.

You stand and look at your mad-tongued kelpie, who barks for the sprinklers to start, but when nothing happens comes up beside you. And shakes himself dry. More laughter. Your children, little chests half heaving with laughter and searching for breath.

I pick up my youngest from where they lie giggling on the ground. Hold her up and all she says is, 'So happy.'

We walk back to our home, where we will find my wife and their mother, and how she will laugh when we tell her of our magic.

And I stand there on the patio and I can almost hear their laughter, feel their hands in mine and how I long for that moment again.

When magic was found on a summer arvo. That moment before life would play out. Where no fear, no sadness, no loss, no broken dreams or hopes dashed, where none of the things that take place through all lives would have yet happened.

Every person, every parent, has probably had that thought and yet we also know that it's just a wish. Life goes on, we go with it. We grow older. We know there will be laughter as well as sadness, wins and losses and life.

And one of the wonders of life is that we have such memories. Such golden lovely memories that come to us when a summer sound unlocks our kitbag.

I opened my eyes and listened to that laughter of the children somewhere in one of the yards below.

And I smiled and realised the cool change had come.

9

THE FESTIVAL OF SUMMER

Summer, being the time of bounty, when the saddlebags of life are full, is the perfect time to celebrate such good fortune and I suppose Christmas and New Year are a part of that celebration, along with the obvious religious significance to those who believe or are reminded of their faith.

But does the time of bounty also cause celebration and festival because of its character?

The things that go through your head when you fill up a car at a petrol station. I don't usually think about 'times of bounty', which sounds like the title of a really bad romance novel, but I was on my way to a celebration of sorts.

A festival.

So, I could be cut a bit of slack for thinking of such things, as I filled up the old tank with diesel. How much longer would I be doing that, I thought. The time had come to embrace yet another phase of life, the transition into EV ownership.

A part of me would miss standing and filling the car, if for no other reason than because filling the car was one of the few practical tasks I could accomplish. It was a hard-earned level of handiness. For example, I had to work through not knowing what the arrow on the petrol gauge symbol meant in the car until I was enlightened by a rather annoyed driver of a LandCruiser. This particular individual had had enough of me trying to determine whether the bowser hose would extend to the other side of the car. So he helpfully pointed out, with a few colourful adjectives, what I should do. As I was humming a song at the time, this seemed to increase the colour of the adjectives slightly and he beeped his horn like a battleship sounding action stations and bellowed, 'Mate, know the geography of your vehicle and the servo.'

'Sorry?' I said.

'There's a little triangle on one side of the fuel indicator that tells you what side your bloody petrol tank is!'

'Oh, thanks.' And I hummed and got back in the car and determined this was in fact correct. That little triangle! Oh, I thought it was an arrow! I got out and gave him a thumbs-up and drove around a bit to align the tank with the bowser.

No need for such skills back in the days when an attendant at the servo would come out and fill the car, wash the windscreen and check your oil for you.

I have a mate who remembers these service days with a sad fondness. He told me once that when he was a boy he used to drive to the same service station with his father. How he had always thought the servo a happy place, where his father and the owner and his staff all chatted happily with each other, talked sport perhaps and asked after each other's families and what the news might be.

Ever since that time, my pal said, even when he has a thousand things on his plate and is in a hurry and wants to get the car filled and get going, there is also a nagging small sadness. As if he has lost something.

'I suppose I have really,' he'd said. 'That chance to be a part of a community. No big thing, but I miss it or the possibility of it.'

I thought of his words when I went in to pay. There was the attendant, an Indian fellow.

I had been driving a while and it was hot, summer hot, but nonetheless I decided to have a chat to the attendant.

He said hello.

I almost shouted hello in return.

He winced. I may have even frightened him.

How was he going? I heard myself bark at him.

'Good,' he said softly.

He told me the required total to be paid.

I asked him if he'd enjoyed the cricket Tests between India and Australia.

He said nothing.

'Great games,' I declared.

He repeated the total.

For some reason, from some part of my memory, I uttered a question that I remembered Ken Macrohan, who ran the BP servo up on the corner of McDonald Road and Oxley Avenue, and my father would take turns asking each other when my father filled up his trucks.

'Got much on for the day?' I enquired enthusiastically.

The attendant just stared.

'I'm going to a festival . . . in Parkes,' I offered.

I could sense I was fading badly but tried to rally with a truly idiotic attempt to bring my thoughts to a public audience, 'Summer, the time of bounty?'

'Please, please,' was all he said in response.

I gave up and paid, lamely asked for a receipt and stomped back to the car.

In much the same tone I had used when trying to recreate that sense of community, I bellowed at my pal in the car, Leo, 'I have just made a complete fucking arse of myself.'

'How and with whom?' asked Leo.

'I just tried to chat with that bloke behind the counter and he behaved like I was trying to abduct him or come on to him or convert him. Fucking bizarre.'

Leo said nothing, then burst out laughing. 'Did you sound like you sound now?'

I admitted I did.

'Well, Will, you may have been giving off a very hairy and cranky Skipper from *Gilligan's Island* vibe. That could be slightly alarming to somebody working in a servo on the register. Was he Indian?'

'I think he was.'

'So he probably wouldn't even be familiar with the Skipper from *Gilligan's Island*. It was just big loud white-guy patter. What else did you say to him?'

I told Leo how I'd posed the idea that summer was a time of bounty.

He exploded with laughter. 'He probably thought you wanted to abduct, come on to and convert him!'

'Oh shut up,' I said, and laughed.

We started saying to each other, 'Summer, a time for bounty?' in stupid accents. Just arsing about.

'It sounds like an ad for a chocolate bar, that Bounty choccy bar,' said Leo.

This made us repeat the phrase even more, with variations which amused us. 'Summer, a time of Bounty. And a time of desiccated coconut!'

I told Leo that the bounty thing was something my mother used to say.

'Ah. Iris. She said many things,' he said.

'Indeed, she did, God love her.'

'God love her,' repeated Leo.

I went on to say that because summer was –

'A time of BOUNTY!' Leo roared and laughed.

'Yes, but that's why people think they have to celebrate it, that's why they have festivals.'

'So?' asked Leo. 'What's the point?'

'Well, what is a festival?'

'It's a festival.'

'Yeah, but what is a festival, is there a definition?'

Leo got on his phone while we had some connection and sifted through definitions of festivals.

'Here we go, this is from the office of the Arts and Festivals Australia. "The Festivals Australia Guidelines define a festival as a program of events that is open to the public and provides an opportunity to gather and celebrate . . ." ' he trailed off and then we both roared, 'A time of BOUNTY!'

Our trip had found its catchphrase.

Summer then seemed the perfect time for festivals and there were more than you could poke a stick at: arts events like the Adelaide Fringe and Adelaide Festival and the Sydney Mardi Gras were among the biggest of their types in the world; Mardi Gras alone attracting hundreds of thousands of people from all over the globe and the Adelaide events selling well over a million tickets.

Music festivals were everywhere too, from the Woodford Folk Festival in Queensland to the Falls Festival and Bluesfest in Byron Bay, the St Kilda Festival, Lost Paradise Festival, Beyond the Valley and the Tamworth Country Music Festival.

Leo used to hit them pretty hard, but he told me those days were long behind him now.

'Most of the time you've got to camp and are locked into a site. There's lots of noise, and those awful portaloos – of which there are never enough – and you're whacked or drunk or both and it's usually over thirty degrees. It's a recipe for disaster.' After a short while he added, 'Or a ripping good time if you are up for it.'

I remember when I was very young and watching a television show called *GTK* – Get to Know – on the ABC with my family. It featured a story about the Sunbury music festivals that were held for a time on part of a farm out in Sunbury, west of Melbourne.

It was supposed to be Australia's answer to Woodstock, but on a black-and-white TV it looked hot and dry and barren. People seemed to be having a good time, but I had to agree with my mother who muttered, 'Where do they bathe, and sleep and do their business?'

Nobody said anything for a bit until my eldest sister offered, 'Well, they must manage, they're enjoying themselves.'

All my mother said was, 'Manky, manky Sunbury.'

The organisers weren't charged a cent by the farmer, who thought that as long as things didn't get too out of hand and people enjoyed themselves, he was more than willing to accommodate the event for nearly five years.

What a good bloke.

Sunbury was out in the sticks back then, but now it's more of a suburb. Every time I am heading out to Tullamarine Airport and see the sign indicating the turnoff to Sunbury, I mutter to myself, 'Manky, manky Sunbury.'

Festivals. I told Leo that my boy had been to music festivals recently and had seen Cheap Trick, the old 1980s party band, play four times.

'Maybe he's a fan,' said Leo.

'I don't think so, there's just so many festivals now that it becomes a circuit and a couple of old acts fill the classic retro spot.'

'As long as people enjoy themselves,' said Leo. 'And why wouldn't they? Everybody loves music.'

That seemed important. Enjoying yourself. I remember going to the Western Port festival, which was held around the town of Hastings in Victoria, nearly a decade ago. There was a street parade on the main drag and a school's float appeared: a long ship plonked on the back of some parent's truck. It was full of Vikings and the odd King Harold with an arrow sticking out of his eye. As well as that mayhem there were a couple of John Colemans, the great Essendon full forward who had lived in Hastings in his youth and whose rather glorious statue stands in front of the local library.

I don't know if there were any Vikings at the Battle of Hastings back in 1066. I am pretty sure poor old Harold turned up, but the great Bomber John Coleman?

It didn't matter because seeing a John Coleman handballing to one of the said King Harolds, then stooping to pick up a Viking hat and return it to its owner before accepting a handball back from old arrow-eye Harold made me laugh in delight.

As long as people enjoy themselves. And I suppose music helps.

It certainly does on a road trip.

Leo and I had been driving for what seemed like ages. Driving long distances is fun in a torturous sort of way. You remember those long-haul trips of your youth when setting out with your family was a mixture of excitement and trepidation. It was a bit like an annual Burke and Wills trip: at the beginning there was the equivalent of brass bands, streamers and excitement as you set off weighted down with all sorts of belongings. And then something was always left behind.

We once had to turn back because we couldn't leave without a colander. My mother had left it on the tray of one of my father's trucks. 'We can't travel without a colander!'

Why, I had no idea.

And just like Burke and Wills, you knew you'd get lost sooner or later. The poor sod chosen to be navigator with a map or a copy of Gregory's Street Directory would be trying to direct a volcanic parent with no idea where we were headed, the Gregory's being turned around on the lap like a roulette wheel in search of the lucky numbers.

None of that for me now. I had a GPS primed, a car that could half drive itself and various digital devices which spoke in that passive voice that is supposedly without a hint of emotion to keep you honest.

The problem started when I began singing. It seems so unjust that whenever I sing in a car somebody puts on the radio, a CD or device. Even I've been known to do it when I've heard myself sing.

It was a passable Dean Martin effort, but my pal Leo muttered, 'This is why we have playlists.'

We chugged along, listening to an eighties playlist. This was somewhat confronting because a sense of mortality descends at the fact you were around to hear these songs the first time. It is why I can remember lyrics to 'The Final Countdown' by Europe, and 'Africa' by Toto and even Depeche Mode.

And Yazoo. Why did I remember the lyrics to the super soppy 'Only You'?

Why?

'Just go with it,' I told myself.

And then, on a road trip, you've got to contend with other motorists. I'm not the best driver but some people seem completely oblivious to cause and effect. They speed and slalom through lanes in their cocooned automotive bubbles without heed.

A little hatchback driven by a P-plater with two pixie figures stuck on the back flew past, over the limit. And a truck, with a transport company brand name plastered over it like a rash, did the same; the driver giving a bit of advice with various fingers to other drivers.

And then the traffic slowed. Roadworks? No. Speed check. We filed past and there parked on the side of the road was the pixie car and the truck. A police officer taking details. The drivers sullen-faced. And as we're crawling past with 'Only You' playing, the copper turned, then pointed at our car. 'Good song!' he said.

If I could have offered anything to the grumpy drivers it would only be to say, 'Music helps.'

The summer lends itself to long drives through 'the sticks' and the towns, even though you have to leave the highways to visit such places. It's another world on the highways; they are purpose-built to simply get you somewhere. The service centres that dot the concrete express lanes are a collection of signs, bowsers, fast food counters and toilets or 'facilities' which see so much traffic above the bowls and before the urinals that they give both great relief and great despair in almost equal quantity.

And these places see such an amazing contrasts in the ways people locomote through the premises.

If you are paying for petrol or gas, you are orderly, in and out, although there are always the receipt checkers who suddenly stop, usually in doorways, to carefully go through the costings like some archaeologist studying the Dead Sea Scrolls.

The food courters are usually lounging, perhaps stretching legs and arms, or staring balefully into a cup of coffee thinking about how far they have to go. Or how far they have travelled.

Then there are the scurriers, people who have only one thought – to get to the 'facilities'. They walk either like a shoplifter, hunched over with effort trying to get away as soon as possible, or like doctors walking purposefully to surgery.

Once I was accused of walking like The Terminator to the toilets. True, my knees were quite stiff from driving, but I moved as quickly as I could to my desired destination in a very well-fed Arnold Schwarzenegger manner.

When I returned, I felt a bit more relaxed and told my travelling companion, in my best bad Arnie/Terminator accent, that after what I had deposited in the facilities, 'I won't be back.'

I remember one place in Gympie that was so sparingly arranged with empty spears that were, I suppose, there for the toilet paper that I had thoughts only of the Spanish Inquisition.

Luckily, I didn't need to use any paper but, on my way, out, even though shaken to my core, I asked the person behind the counter if she knew there wasn't any paper in 'there'.

She looked at me a moment and said with a slight smile, 'Oh, paper? You must ask for paper.'

I wondered how many people had got in there, and once over their shock of what it looked like, had done their business and had found themselves with no paper.

She must have read my thoughts, and she said with an even bigger smile, 'Oh, there is a sign,' and she pointed to the door.

I walked over to where she pointed and, to be sure, on a Post-it-sized note, in small uneven letters was, 'Ask for paper.'

I nodded.

Long trips can be fraught, especially when you're travelling through the sticks, but sometimes those summer drives to the sticks can be good for the soul and put things in perspective. Although sometimes it can take a while to find some country. I remember heading out to Kingaroy along the D'Aguilar Highway. When I was a kid, Caboolture was country, now it's a collection of never-ending concrete malls and suburbs. I passed the D'Aguilar Hotel, otherwise known as the 'Dag' pub, and I couldn't believe how much it'd grown or how much the country around it had built up. On past Kilcoy and finally there was a sense of space.

I rolled into Moore, where I stopped, because I'd never stopped there before. I ordered a coffee and a 'famous crab sandwich', which I'd never had before. 'Why are they famous?' I enquired of the woman behind the counter.

'Once you've had 'em, you won't forget 'em,' she said flatly.

Eating a crab sandwich that far inland? It's a roll of the dice but it was 'Fishy Friday', and the dice fell the right way. They were delicious. I told the woman behind the counter the sangers deserve to be famous.

She smiled and said, 'Spread the word and you travel safe.'

On to Kingaroy. The land around was a lovely green, looking like a calendar illustration. The recent rains had worked a bit of cosmetic surgery, but the drought, the hard times, weren't far away. Speaking of being dry, my throat was fairly parched, and I thought of that almost mythical place on road trips – 'a good country pub', up there with a 'good country bakery'.

I found a gem of a pub passing through Wooroolin: The Grand Hotel, not far from the Wooroolin Wetlands. If you wanted a pub that looked like it belonged in the sticks, you wouldn't have to look much further than the Grand. A graceful and airy verandah wraps across the face of the double-level weatherboard pub. Inside, it's even better. I pulled up a seat at the Boggy Creek Bar and sipped my way through two frothies over a half an hour.

There, I experienced something that probably only happens in the sticks. During my visit I shared the Boggy Creek Bar with two other blokes: the barman and a customer sitting down at the other end of the bar. He's an older bloke doing a crossword in a newspaper. The barman occasionally wanders down and sees how the older bloke is going. The older bloke proffers the newspaper, the barman reads a clue, frowns and then the older bloke taps his pen on the newspaper.

He's solved something. The barman smiles and nods.

Nothing is said until the older bloke stands and says simply, 'Thanks for the chat.'

The barman replies, 'Pleasure. Anytime. Travel safe.'

The older bloke gives a thumbs-up and offers me a nod of farewell. I nod back.

Somehow, I feel something more was communicated. Something was shared, a kindness and a care. People can be hard to read sometimes, but there was a generosity in the old Boggy Creek Bar that marked the Grand Hotel as a fairly decent watering hole.

•

The reason for that road trip was because I was speaking at a conference sponsored by Rotary. When I told a mate that this was what I was up to, he laughed.

'Kingaroy and Rotarians! Good luck. What a combo.' And he laughed again.

I suppose you can laugh at Rotarians and service clubs. They all seem to be pretty easy-going so, sure, you can laugh – but not at the work they do, the effort they put in.

The Kingaroy conference was about building stronger communities and reaching out to help. There was talk of sharing stories and each other's lives. It was about trying to understand that not all people are the same and that for some life can be a bit much, that sometimes it's best just to wait and let people talk; to listen and not move on thinking they don't have much to offer.

There were plans to offer mental health services, raise funds for suicide prevention and for local schools. It was a tonic to be a part of a bunch of people getting up and lending a hand.

I was chatting to an engineer from Longreach who summed up the feeling of that weekend in the sticks. 'It's good to stop a moment or two and just see how things settle. Make sure nobody's being left too far behind. Not too much to ask, we've just got to remember to bloody do it occasionally, that's the trick to it.'

My phone was full of messages and emails and voicemails all wanting me to be somewhere soon and doing something else. Business to attend to, things that couldn't wait and decisions that had to be made. Or did they? It's good to stop a moment or two and see how things settle.

Heading back to Brisbane airport, I stopped for one of life's great delights: a pie from the Blackbutt Bakery. As good as ever. Then a police car roared past, then an ambulance and then the firies.

263

A crash on the road out of town, the road to Brisbane. That meant the road would close.

I had a car to return, a plane to catch.

'Might miss your flight, Will,' said another pie-fancier who had been at the Kingaroy conference.

On a beautiful Sunday afternoon, after such a lovely, generous weekend, just down the road lives were in peril. The ambos and the police were lending a hand. I knew what was important. And that was the people the first responders were racing to.

'You'll have to wait till the road's open,' said the pie-fancier.

I shrugged. 'Long as they're okay. Always another plane. And it means I can have another pie.'

We laughed.

A trip to the sticks puts things in perspective.

•

Sometimes these summer road trips simply take you to another place to sit and that very act takes you out of yourself.

Leo and I pulled up at an old gold rush town to get a room for the night before completing our trip to the festival the next arvo.

We decided to go off to the local RSL for a bite and a gargle. The town had lovely old art deco buildings and the deep-set solidness of Federation architecture, which look strangely grand for some of the businesses that are found within: a life coaching office, a gym with boutique fitness studios available.

In the RSL there was a gaming room to one side with machines flashing like controls from some bad war movie situation room.

A stream of people were moving to and from the situation room.

We ordered food and a beer and saw that there was cricket on one television screen and beside it another monitor displaying Australian military history for the month of January.

We looked at both. We saw a burly middle-order player belt a ball for six in a Twenty20 game and on the other screen we learned that the aircraft carrier HMAS *Sydney* began its last tour of duty in the waters off Korea during the Korean War.

The television showed a replay of a man in the crowd dropping a catch of the burly middle-order batsman's six. The man shook his hands as well as his head.

Albert Jacka received his Victoria Cross for acts of valour during the First World War and the other screen showed a four racing to the boundary while flames erupted and some awkward dancers gyrated on a platform erected at the Twenty20.

The burly batsman lifted his bat to acknowledge the crowd's applause for his 'fighting fifty'.

Then the monitor informed us that January saw the peak of Australian involvement in the Vietnam War, with the deployment of 8900 service men and women.

There was a break in the cricket and a car ad came on.

'This is a bit odd, these two screens,' said Leo. 'I wonder if Albert Jacka knew he was fighting for bad dancing, junk cricket and overpriced monster utes.'

'It's a part of what Australia's become, and back in his day he fought for Australia to be what it wanted,' I said.

'Fair call,' said Leo. 'I wouldn't hold Jacka VC responsible for any of that stuff. Just makes you think.'

I nodded.

The situation-room gaming machines clattered and chimed and their lights went off. Young blokes walked past our table.

One, still in his fluoro work clothes, said, 'I was up and now I'm down.'

'That's a night on the punt, mate,' said another.

'Yeah, but now I'm down,' said the fluoro-clad night-on-the-punter.

Then some bloke tilted his chair too far back and fell, hitting his head on the floor.

He was tended to by staff and a couple of off-duty nurses who were having dinner with their families.

'Funny,' said Leo, 'we're having a beer, they're having dinner, they were having a night on the punt and he's having his head tended to.' He flicked his beer in the direction of the bloke who'd met the floor with force. 'And there's those names on the wall.'

He looked up at an honour roll of remembrance to the fallen. 'Makes you think.'

I nodded again. 'You can only live when you live.'

Leo looked at me and I told him that's what my mum used to say.

'Ah, Iris. God love her.' And he raised his glass.

'God love her.' I raised my glass and said, 'And here's to Albert Jacka, to people on the punt, to people helping out and to the names on the wall and to things that make you think.'

Leo nodded.

Then he asked me why I had tried to make friends with the servo attendant.

'I wasn't trying to make friends with him,' I said a little too loudly and a few heads turned, including that of the man who had hit his head and one of the nurses who were tending to him. Leo smiled and I lowered my voice and told him about my other pal's memory of service stations.

Leo nodded as if my pal had a point, then he said, quite cannily, 'Did your mate ever try to go into a modern self-serve and talk to the people there as if it were 1974?'

I said I didn't know, but I would make sure to find out, and we laughed.

We finished our drinks, looked at each other and said, 'Summer, a time of bounty!'

•

The establishment we stayed in that night was one of those places that you only seem to visit when embarking on a summer adventure to a festival. The sort of place that would get five stars on a serial killer's Tripadvisor site. To call it grim was an understatement, but on the upside at least we didn't have to ask for paper. This was a bonus as our host was a slightly confronting fellow.

When we checked in, he came to the reception window and stared intently. He was wearing a singlet and had Brylcreemed hair. As soon as I went to say something he started speaking – so our conversation was like watching a bad session from Question Time in the House of Representatives; in other words, people talking over each other.

It was like he was trying to read my mind and anticipate my question before I'd finished asking it and so he would start talking about something completely unconnected to what I wanted to know.

I even slipped in a 'Summer, a time of bounty!' when I asked what the checkout time was, and he was talking about where to put used towels.

A natural for the service industry.

So, when the time came, we bade a fond farewell to Norman Bates' Antipodean nephew with a wave and a friendly toot on the car's horn. He just stood in his singlet and shorts and stared.

On to the festival. If you thought Vikings, Eye-on-the-arrow King Harold and John Coleman had little in common, then try figuring out how an odd momma's boy from Memphis came to have a statue of himself erected in a position of prominence in a small town in western New South Wales.

The Parkes Elvis Festival. How did it start and why did I want to go?

In 1992 a couple who had never managed to visit Elvis's old home Graceland on a trip to the States made up for that fact by owning the restaurant 'Graceland' in town and were hosting a birthday party for a member of a local family.

One of the members was a local journalist who, like the rest of his clan, were rabid Elvis Presley fans. The King of Rock'n'roll's hits were played into the night and, over a glass of red wine, the idea of having a week of Elvis celebrations was planted.

They tried to find a date and came up with early January. The high temperatures drove locals to the beach and business was quiet – some places even shutting up shop. Early January happened to be Elvis Aaron Presley's birthday, so it was set and the next year a humble event took place. And it never looked back.

These days the event attracts over 25,000 visitors and festival guest. In a town of just over 10,000 citizens, the place stretches to bursting point. It turns an amazing amount of coin for the community and raises large sums for a local charity, so where is the downside? Someone could find one, I'm sure, but why bother?

Parkes is also the location of the radio telescope that played a pivotal role in the Moon landing in 1969. And in the town's central public garden there is one of my favourite pieces of civic sculpture: Jaffa the Astronaut. It was created by the Sydney art studio Amigo & Amigo, and the three-metre orange astronaut sculpture pays tribute to the diverse and under-appreciated heroes of space travel, from astronauts to mathematicians and beyond. The Parkes Shire Council bought it to mark the fiftieth anniversary of Parkes' successful role in broadcasting images of the *Apollo 11* Moon landing around the world.

At the other end of the park is the statue of Elvis Presley, dressed in his Vegas Elvis garb. It looks like he has just slipped a disc as, even though he's smiling, he's bending over at an ungainly and rather immodest angle. Never mind, both statues feature in a lot of photos.

Why did I want to go? Early in January some years ago my brother phoned me in a state of great mirth and left a message as follows: 'Bill, Vaughan. Mate, mate. MATE. Am at the Parkes Elvis do with Angus and Louie. I am at the trots; it is pissing down and there is a flat-top truck driving around with about five Elvises on the tray taking turns to sing into loud hailers. It is delightful bedlam. A-grade arsing about. Grab some mates and make sure you make it here at least once.'

So, I had to go – at least once. To see the Dish, Jaffa and Elvis and his festival friends. This was the year. This was the season. 'Summer, a time of bounty!'

At our accommodation we caught up with another of our festival party, Niall, just in time to get to the trots.

As far as festivals go, it was love at first flutter. I love a punt and as we walked into the Parkes Paceway, we were met with the sight of a fleet of a thousand Grey Nomad Schooners – Winnebago motorhomes.

It became apparent the festival catered to the older demographic, although there were people of varying ages around. A sign displayed out the front of the paceway, which belonged to a certain religious group, proudly boasted, 'The King appeals to all.'

It was here at the Parkes Paceway that we saw our first Elvis – a bloke in a big wig, makeup, a dark suit and in fine voice. It was a little Attenborough-esque, as if we were searching for a species of wildlife that flocked together in this particular part of the earth for mating or some such ritual.

This Elvis sounded like Elvis when he sang, but he spoke like a golfer, with a funny trans-Pacific accent that professional athletes often get when they spend time between America and Australia.

He sang some tunes, got cut off mid-song with the words from the race-caller, 'Sorry, King, we've got to go for the fifth – and they're away!'

He took this in good grace and, when the race was over, simply picked up the song from where he had left off. There was also a moment when he asked where people had come from. From Queensland, Victoria, Tasmania and New Zealand – basically from all over Australasia.

When Trots Elvis asked if anyone was from overseas, a man put his arm up.

'Where have you come from, man?' asked Trots Elvis.

'Holland,' yelled the man.

'Holland!' said Trots Elvis.

'Thirty years ago!' yelled the man.

'Thirty years ago, and you just got here – they tell me the parking is bad at the trots but at least you made it.' This Elvis was fun.

He asked the man his name.

'Roff!' he shouted.

Elvis Trots stared.

'Roff! Roff!' shouted the man again.

'Hey, man, settle down, you'll have all the dogs in Parkes gong off!'

There was laughter. The man apologised and said he was a little hard of hearing, that's why he shouted.

Elvis Trots said he was sorry. 'I shouldn't have said that, sir.'

Roff shouted back, 'No, no, don't say sorry, this is fun.'

Elvis Trots asked if Roff would like to hear a song.

Somebody else said, 'Sing "Wooden Heart"!'

Elvis Trots held up his hand, 'Hey, it's a German song and he's Dutch, there's a bit of history there, maybe Roff Roff would like to hear "Hound Dog"?'

And this delightful fellow looked over to Roff and said, 'Sorry, couldn't help myself.'

Roff laughed along with his wife and yelled out, 'Thank you, Elvis man, but the puppet song is good, I like it.'

Elvis Trots nodded and said, 'Roff, this one is for you.' And as he sang 'Wooden Heart', people sang along.

That moment was a template for that funny old festival: good humour, a little care and generosity. People enjoying themselves.

There were too many highlights. We were joined by boon companions Simon and Anthony the Trick Cyclist as he was a psychiatrist of some note.

I asked Anthony if he was here to study in a professional capacity and he replied with a smile, 'Brother, I am off duty and just here for the parade! Even bought a special suit. One hundred per cent of the finest polyester.'

The theme of the festival was 'Easy Come, Easy Go' which was an inspired piece of cinematic lameness Elvis specialised in during his film career. The plot was a beauty: a former US Navy frogman – our old mate Elvis – discovers what may be a fortune in Spanish gold aboard a sunken ship and attempts to retrieve it with the help of a go-go dancing yoga expert.

What more could you ask for? US military, frogman, yoga experts and sunken treasure.

Niall had gone to great effort with a frogman outfit complete with an old weed-spray backpack doubling as his scuba air tanks. I was going to follow suit but thought better and just went in my civvies.

Even Jaffa the Astronaut had gotten into the spirit of things, for someone had placed upon his helmet a pair of goggles and a snorkel and on his space boots, flippers. It was that sort of festival: tongue in cheek and fun.

There was also a statue of the man who the town was named after: Henry Parkes, The Father of Federation. It stood on the corner of Clarinda and Welcome streets, Clarinda being the name of Parkes' wife.

The number of times people looked up and wondered if the statue had something to do with the Elvis Festival was rather surprising.

'That's not the Elvis statue, is it?' asked a woman dressed, I think, as Priscilla.

'No, Elvis never had a beard,' said a man who was in the almost obligatory Elvis costume and who also incidentally had a beard.

'No, wait there, he did have one in *Charro!*.' He paused, thinking. 'But he didn't sing in *Charro!*. It was a Western.'

'How do you know all this crap, Neil?' asked Priscilla.

'Research – I told you I wanted to do well in that Elvis trivia night at the bowlo,' said bearded Neil Presley.

'So who is this guy?' said Priscilla of the statue.

'Don't know, a guy with a beard who's shouting. Looks a bit like Karl Marx.'

Priscilla leaned in and read the plaque. 'It says it's Henry Parkes, not Karl Marx.'

'Henry Parkes! The Father of Federation,' declared Neil Presley.

Priscilla looked at him.

'Remember the trivia night at the school fundraiser?'

Priscilla looked a bit blank and then said, 'I remember that beautiful grenache! Federation?'

'Yeah, when all the colonies got together and became Australia – he was one of the organisers.'

'Right, so he's got nothing to do with the Elvis Festival.'

'No, he's just here all the time,' said Neil, and he and Priscilla walked off.

He's just here all the time. Poor old Henry, I thought, he did look a bit angry, shouting up the street with a book open in one hand while he points with the other. But nobody was listening. It wasn't Henry's weekend; they were here for Elvis.

Not far from Henry 'he's just here all the time' Parkes was a poster featuring a still from the film *Easy Come, Easy Go* showing the King in a naval cap, smiling. It was a great photo because it looked like he was laughing at what was going on. At Henry yelling up the street. Or as if Elvis was just laughing at himself. A lopsided grin, as if he couldn't believe that, nearly sixty years after he was playacting on that film, there was a festival dedicated to such a piece of nonsense.

He looked like he was taking the piss, as if the whole thing was just one huge joke, which was, quite frankly, the best of Elvis and simply marvellous.

We tried to run a book on what was the most played song but gave up because the place was filled with wall-to-wall Elvis warbling, although at last count 'The Wonder of You' seemed to be the frontrunner.

There was an Elvis Art Exhibition that had a few portraits of the King, which all managed a unique feat in that they all resembled the former Australian cricketer, Mark Waugh. I wondered if they were all by the same person.

So, there we were in 35-degrees-plus heat, with people dressed in scuba outfits, some top shelf and some from the Reject shop or its equivalent. There were Elvis costumes in the finest polyester, the occasional naval uniform and the odd 'hippie'. I noticed the op shops stayed open all through the festival and did a boom trade when they would otherwise have been closed.

There was a police officer on active duty, with his police vest and side-arm, and radio, walking the beats dressed head to toe as Elvis.

He was stopped every few steps for a photo.

It was staggeringly hot.

On the main stage, in a variety of pubs and the Leagues club in the middle of the town, Elvises of all shapes and sizes sang, struck poses and sweated with all the shakin' going on.

There was a Kiwi Elvis and an Islander Elvis and an Elvis from the Philippines and a Scottish Elvis who looked like a Bay City Roller. We never saw him perform but he was chatting quite happily with various people, always leaning rather jauntily with his hand on his wheelie suitcase.

There was an Elvis who looked like he had very bad indigestion when he sang and I heard a couple on the next table talking about him.

'Every time he opens his mouth to sing, I think he's going to let out a huge belch.'

'He should be singing "Burp Suede Shoes" instead of "Blue Suede Shoes".'

'Perhaps he should just go to the toilet?'

'Oh God no! That's where Elvises go to die!'

There was an Elvis who was the spit of a cross between Michael Landon from *Little House on the Prairie* and Don West from *Lost in Space*. He sounded like he was off the boat from Taranaki but it didn't matter really, for an Elvis was an Elvis.

I was getting a coffee when I overheard other festival punters chatting about the goings-on. They all had Elvis outfits on.

'It's pretty bogan, isn't it? And very white. But it is fun,' said Elvis number 1.

'That's the whole point. What was Elvis, except a talented bogan who sang other people's songs and looked great doing it? But you're right, it's fun,' said Elvis 2.

I let that settle and then I heard another couple of Elvises dressed in the same get-up talking behind me.

'So, I was in hospital with him and Dad was still fighting, you know,' said Elvis 3.

'I know, he is a tough old coot,' replied Elvis 4.

'And he said to me, "I've made it my goal to live another year,"' said Elvis 3.

'Yeah? Hey, is it a latte you want?' asked Elvis 4.

'Yes, mate, thanks. And I look at him and I just say "Why? You are wearing a fucking nappy. Just die,"' said Elvis 3.

'You said that?' asked Elvis 4.

'Yeah, and he looked at me and said, "Fair point."'

'He said that?' said Elvis 4.

'Yeah. Hey, he'll love that photo you took of that Priscilla and me. I'll show him when I see him on Tuesday at the hospital,' said Elvis 3.

'No worries, mate. It was a latte, wasn't it?' said Elvis 4.

I was still taking that in when it was my turn to order. When I was asked what I would like I had to pause for a moment.

The person behind the counter then said to me, 'Excuse me, have you come as the Colonel?'

I stared back for I had no idea what she was talking about. The Colonel? Did she mean Colonel Sanders?

'Sorry?' I said.

'The Colonel. Have you come as Colonel Tom Parker? That is so brave. I have never seen a Colonel Tom Parker here before. Good on you, I guess.'

I wasn't dressed as anything other than myself. It was too hot for my scuba outfit, so I had simply plonked a broad-brimmed sunhat on my nonce. The rest was just my usual wardrobe, and I had been congratulated on my Colonel Tom Parker costume.

I got my coffee and said thanks.

'No worries, Colonel.'

I was mulling this 'Colonel' business over when I saw another pair of Elvises – do they always travel in pairs? I wondered – who were huddled around a bin trying to dispose of their takeaway food containers in the phalanx of rubbish bins all lined up with different coloured lids to denote what should go where. It seemed the two Kings were having a little difficulty working out where what should indeed go.

'No, this blue is for recycling, that coffee cup, that's not recycling. Is it?' said the larger Elvis.

'Well, it's got the little arrows on the bottom, doesn't that mean it's recycling?' said the smaller Elvis who, I realised, was female. Good for her I thought, nice to see someone not being pushed into the obvious Priscilla path or Go-Go dancers or the contentious 'Hippies/Yoga People'.

The male Elvis took off his glasses. 'Oh, I can't see anything with these things on.' And he lifted the cup to see the little arrows on the bottom.

'Oh, watch it, Barry!' said the female Elvis. 'You're spilling it everywhere.'

As Barry the Male Elvis lifted up the coffee cup to see the little arrows, he indeed was spilling out the remaining dregs of coffee in the cup.

It fell on his legs.

'Oh blow,' he said.

'You're like a toddler, Barry! You got food all over yourself and now the coffee!' said the female Elvis.

Barry Elvis dropped his glasses and then threw the coffee cup in the landfill bin. 'No, you can't recycle them, there is a film of plastic around the inside. Landfill, seems a waste.'

I bent down and picked up his gold plastic Elvis Specs and then waited to give them back to him.

'I am a bit of a mess aren't I, darl?'

He presented himself to the female Elvis and she laughed. 'You look like something out of a Freddy Krueger slasher movie.'

He did indeed look like something out of Nightmare on Elvis Street. His jumpsuit had crimson and black stains all over the front.

'That's the sweet 'n' sour pork and then that bit is the soy. The dim sims were very good and those little dumplings.'

'God, Barry, you don't have to go through everything that you've spilt on yourself,' said Darl Elvis. 'You eat the way Jackson Pollock painted.'

And she laughed.

'You know, normal people just take photos on their phones to remember what they've done. You have to create a work of art.'

Barry shrugged his Elvis shoulders and smiled back. 'I'll pop off to the ablution block at the showgrounds and put the Elvis gear through the wash tonight so I'm a blank canvas for tomorrow.'

Darl laughed a little again. 'That's a bit of a shame, I quite like this Pollock you're wearing today.'

'"Ablution Block" sounds like an Elvis song, instead of "Jailhouse Rock"!' cried Barry and then he sang, epically out of tune, 'Come to the Ablution Block with me and let's wash!' to the tune of 'Jailhouse Rock'.

Darl smiled, and then saw me holding Barry's glasses.

'Barry, this man has got your glasses.'

Barry stopped singing, turned, said sorry and then thank you.

I told him it was no problem and that he should find a free microphone and belt out 'Ablution Block'.

He put his glasses on and said the obligatory 'Thank you very much' in a passable Elvis voice and I walked on. Humming 'Ablution Block'!

It was that sort of summer day. Two Elvises trying to work out the recycling, and somehow the combination of Jackson Pollock and the King of Rock'n'roll co-mingling beautifully with new lyrics to an old classic.

The other startling thing I noticed as I walked back with my coffee was that many of the Elvises in costume disturbingly resembled the plank-faced former Australian cricketing all-rounder Shane Watson, which slightly perplexed me. What was this relationship between Elvis Presley and former Australian cricketers?

When I got back to the rest of the crew, I told Niall what the coffee lady said to me about coming as Colonel Tom Parker.

'The Colonel? Will, do you think the universe is trying to tell you something?'

I said I didn't know but maybe the coffee lady and the Universe had a point, and I looked around the park at all the Elvises and suddenly thought to myself, what would be the plural of Elvis?

'Elvi' sounded good to me, so I shared this with Niall, who obligingly nodded with a smile. I spotted two Elvi walking not too far away holding hands, Darl and Barry Nightmare on Elm Street Elvis – so I told Niall about the 'Ablution Block Rock'.

He laughed. Hummed the tune then sang a bar or two. '"The Ablution Block Rock",' he said. 'That is a definite earworm.'

Then he furrowed his brow and said, 'Is it Amenities Block or Ablution Block? Amenities or Ablution?'

'Perhaps Amenities is the Greek god of Ablutions?'

'Or Ablutions is the Greek god of Amenities?'

'I suppose it's all about how you look at your Greek mythology.'

'And going to the dunny.'

'Indeed,' I said and then I laughed.

'The ablution block,' said Niall. 'Now that is a sound of summer, mate.'

'Going to the dunny?' I asked.

'Indeed,' he said, mimicking me. 'When I was a kid, we had a caravan at the old park in Busselton next to the cemetery – what a place for a caravan park!'

He laughed. 'And whenever one of us kids went off to the toilet, one of our parents would yell out, 'Wear your thongs to the ablution block!!' And all the other parents would yell the same thing when their kids went, so the caravan park by the cemetery was full of that cry, "Wear your thongs to the ablution block!"'

'That is a sound of summer! And it stank too! The piss trough had these blocks of antiseptic or cleaner or whatever – and they stank, but they weren't like the round little ones, you used to get. No, these things were like jagged bits of rock. Blue. Like icebergs – bigger than the one that sank the *Titanic*.'

He shook his head.

I looked at the Elvi and after a little I said, 'I like Busselton. I like the jetty.'

Niall didn't say anything for a moment and then said softly, 'I know you do, Tall Timber.' And a moment later, he asked, 'Did Sarah like Elvis?'

I glanced at him and he was looking at the Elvi but listening.

Sarah, my wife. I said, 'Yes, she did, I suppose, in a round-about way. She thought he was a bit of fun.'

'That sounds right.' And he patted me gently on the hand, all the while looking at the assembled Elvi.

It was one of those moments when you understand how lovely it is to have old friends. People who can read between your words, know where your thoughts might lead, under-stand that, sometimes, you might be more than just a large foghorn of a man.

Like knowing how that lovely jetty, that finger above the sea makes me think of those who have left me.

Such moments are filled with unspoken kindness, generosity and warmth. Moments, letting you know that you are not alone. It is quite frankly one of the joys of being human, if you are fortunate enough to have old friends who know you. Good friends.

But just to prove that I am also a very large foghorn of a man, I howled at Niall.

He shrieked a little and looked startled.

'Niall, where has your Elvis frogman cozzie gone?' I cried, adding a bellow to my howl.

Elvi heads turned accusingly.

'Jesus, Colonel, give me a break,' said Niall. 'Mate, too friggin' hot. I made a donation to St Vinnies, and I think it was snapped up by that bloke there.'

Niall pointed to an Elvis in a polyester jumpsuit who had all the accoutrements of Niall's outfit. 'I wonder if I should tell him there is still Round-up in the spray pack.'

I looked at him. 'Just joking, it's DDT,' he deadpanned, and we laughed.

It was hot.

So hot that we nearly lost Anthony the Trick Cyclist when he was wearing his 100 per cent polyester suit.

'I am evaporating in this bloody thing,' he croaked.

'You look a bit like Marty McFly's brother and sister disappearing in the photographs,' Simon helpfully added, referencing *Back to the Future*.

'Come on, none of that pseudo-Freudian stuff, I'm just evaporating.'

We went to the Leagues club with its air-conditioned comfort and its roll call of continuous Elvis performers.

It was there I saw the something that was quite wonderful.

The Elvis performing sang an old sweet Elvis number called 'Follow That Dream', a wonderful piece of supreme early sixties pop. Simplistic, melodious; such a well-crafted piece of music but with sweet lyrics and such a light and soaring sentiment about following your dream to find a love you need.

The whole place lifted. Human beings of seemingly every shape and size, some in costume, some not, some old, some young, some disabled, some obviously with serious health issues – all seemed astoundingly happy. Smiles were everywhere.

Niall appeared with a beer in his hand and dressed only in the hint of his frogman, he looked like someone going for a swim in the 1890s. He stood and he laughed. 'They are so fucking happy.' And he toasted the room.

The Trick Cyclist reappeared, non-evaporated, and he stared in genuine wonder. 'My goodness,' he said, a smile spreading across his face. 'This is what a great day looks like.'

Simon asked him if it was his professional opinion.

He just smiled.

Leo stood next to me and said, 'There's your answer, Will.'

I asked him what he meant.

'Your answer to what is a festival.' And he gestured to the room.

I laughed. And as the Elvis did an encore of that magical song, just to keep the feeling in the room going because it was so marvellous, Leo said to the room, 'Summer, a time of bounty!'

Indeed.

10

THE LAST DAYS OF SUMMER

Down the beach where I live there is a sure sign that summer is coming to an end. A local family has for years parked a pontoon just off the beach not too far from where the creek runs into the bay waters.

Originally it was used to service their big catamaran, the *Simba*, which would occasionally be anchored there when they would sail it from the yacht club where it was usually harboured.

And when the pontoon goes, so does summer.

The pontoon had become a part of the character of the beach over all the summers it has been there and as a beach belongs to the people, so the pontoon stopped being one family's belonging. People of all ages would swim out to it. Some used it as a marker to reach and then return from on their daily swim. Others would swim out to it and just loll about, lying flat on the platform as it floated in the waves.

Kids would swim out there and jump up on it and then out from it, legs and arms flailing, before splashing in the water. It had been a part of the beach for years, but as the local talk had it, the shire council wasn't too happy with it and wanted it gone.

Perhaps they had their reasons, but it seemed petty because the family had long since stopped anchoring their yacht there and just put out the pontoon during the summer for those locals and visitors who had grown used to its presence.

It was a way of helping keep the character of this pleasant village by the beach where we lived.

'They don't care about stuff like that, do they?' said a woman who I was on nodding terms with as we walked our dogs along the sand.

'I hope it comes back next year,' I said.

She made a small wistful sound. 'That's about all we can do. I wrote a letter to the shire, never got a reply.'

It was my turn to make a small sound.

'No, I don't think they really care,' was all she said, and she walked off.

I looked out at the spot where the pontoon had been moored. Summer was ending and I felt a little odd.

I think it was just that time was passing and, even though it is hard sometimes to note the changing of seasons in Australia, it's there.

The mornings were growing darker and there was a golden tinge to the evenings telling you autumn was on the way. And nature seemed to explode one last time before the season was out, bugs and insects going into overdrive, eucalypts blossoming one last glorious time and a variety of birds knocking themselves out having a roaring good time in their branches.

There is a beautiful gum tree that borders my place, a towering thing that is comfortably the size of an office building.

When it flowered, with those tiny buds of eucalypt gold, and its bark peeling, a colony of corellas got a bit carried away ripping at the gum and its branches. And showering what lay below in a continuous avalanche of detritus.

What lay beneath was my backyard.

Almost every day the pool filled up with so much litter that it began to look like a large soup.

I dutifully tried to remove the worst of it each morning with a telescopic pole and a skimmer net. It became a complete drag and, quite frankly, a shitty way to start the day.

One morning, not long after the pontoon had disappeared for another year, I stood in my PJs and slippers, grumbling as I dragged the skimmer net through the wreckage of the corellas.

When I splashed too much water on my slippers, I yelled at the tree, 'You arsehole of a thing!'

The tree didn't seem to care.

So, I had a go at the corellas. 'Blue-eyed bloody pests.'

They just screeched. Obviously they could give as good as they got.

I looked down at my soaked slippers and something caught my eye.

Something odd.

A wasp, black and yellow and seriously large, was grappling with a large huntsman spider. The spider must have come from the palm trees that surround the pool. The two things rolled over each other in a tangle of legs and wings and fangs.

This is the end of summer, I thought. It was disturbingly ferocious and I reached into my pocket and extricated my phone.

I typed in 'spider-eating wasp'. Simplistically literal but up it popped. There is a thing called a spider-eating wasp and it arcs up near the end of summer. It was all there on a state government website. 'Female wasps prepare nest chambers by dragging spiders to a burrow in the ground, on tree trunks or a nest made out of mud. They paralyse spiders by stinging them and an egg is laid on the spider's body. The larva hatches and feeds internally on the spider's bodily fluids.'

'Jesus,' I said to myself. It was like something out of Ridley Scott's film *Alien*. 'You old dog, Ridley, you just ripped off a spider wasp.'

It was a pretty stark example of life in the backyard.

The wasp wasn't grappling with the spider, it was dragging it in a straight line – they like to do that, apparently – across the pool's paving. It made its way to, and then through, the fence and across a path in the garden to where I assumed its mud nest was situated.

I watched until it and the spider incubator had gone.

I absent-mindedly pulled the skimmer net through the water, like a disinterested gondolier, and then wondered if the canals of Venice were as full of crap as my pool.

Why do I think such silly things?

Then I thought about that spider wasp again, about how odd and how random but how much a part of life that battle with the spider was. Those things, those bugs, were just doing what they do at the end of summer: a battle to survive and procreate. Life.

'Jesus,' I said softly.

Life can be confronting. Fragile. Ugly even. I suddenly had a pang, almost a fear about all those seemingly random events that can befall people. How did I get from yelling at a tree to contemplating mortality?

I shook my head ruefully. What can you do?

The corellas screeched. I looked up at the tree again, but instead of muttering or yelling, I noticed something beautiful. That glorious mighty gum almost shimmering in the sun. A beautiful, messy thing. Just like life, really.

The summer was ending but it would come again. Hopefully the pontoon would return for another summer, another season and a chance to make new memories, enjoy old ones and be with people and things you love. To remember things and those that have passed.

I continued to look at the tree. Life, I thought, is all about perspective. And so I raised my hand and pointed upwards and said to the wonder above, 'Hey, tree, you are all right.'

And I went back to cleaning the pool and humming a tune, that old Elvis song 'Follow That Dream', to farewell summer.

Glorious, lovely, messy summer.

ACKNOWLEDGEMENTS

I would like to acknowledge, in no particular order of importance, the following: Karen Ward, Deonie Fiford, Fiona Hazard, Vanessa Radnidge, all at Hachette, Bernadette Foley, The Fly!, Sahara, Pizza Feet, Bevan Bleakley, Rick McCosker, Paleface Adios, Peter Bolton, Captain Jeremy, Foxy Danbar, Hang On Snoopy, Gigantor, Virgil Tracy, Sir Toby, The Squire, Vaughan, Laurie, Rhian, Corby, Niall Mather, Leo, The Flying Corona, Spiros Arion, Johnny Cougar, Ted Jackson, Bobo Bojangles, Clem McInnes, Gene McInnes, Fi and Merge, The Gazelle, Ray and the little boy on the jetty.

William McInnes is one of Australia's most popular writers and actors. His books include the bestselling memoirs *A Man's Got to Have a Hobby* and *That'd Be Right*. In 2012 his book *Worse Things Happen at Sea*, co-written with his wife, Sarah Watt, was named the best non-fiction title in the ABIA and Indie Book Awards.

Also an award-winning actor and best known for his leading roles in *Blue Heelers*, *SeaChange*, *Total Control*, *NCIS Sydney* and *The Newsreader*, William has won two Logies and two AFI/AACTA Awards for Best Actor in the film *Unfinished Sky* and Best Supporting Actor in *The Newsreader*.

William grew up in Queensland and lives in Melbourne.